You CAN Train
Cat

You CAN Train Your Cat

Secrets of a Master Cat Trainer

Gregory Popovich

St. Martin's Griffin
New York

www.stmartins.com

Researcher/writing coach: Michael Sion, *mikewriter38@earthlink.net*

Photographer: Amy Bloberger, *AOKphotography.com*

Book design by Kathryn Parise

Assistant to Gregory Popovich during the writing of this book:
Alex Dumas

LIBRARY OF CONGRESS CATALOGING-IN-PUBLICATION DATA

Popovich, Gregory.
   You can train your cat : secrets of a master cat trainer / Gregory Popovich.—1st ed.
      p. cm.
   ISBN 978-0-312-56528-2
   1. Cats—Training.   2. Cats—Behavior.   I. Title.
   SF446.6.P67 2009
   636.8'0835—dc22

2009016678

10   9   8   7   6   5

Disclaimer

Gregory Popovich is not a licensed veterinarian, and the information and advice contained in this book should in no way replace the assessment, advice, supervision, and/or care of a licensed veterinarian. Without routine visits to a licensed animal-care practitioner, you are compromising the health of your pet.

For all the people who openly love their cats, and all the cats that secretly love their people

Contents

Part I

Laying the Groundwork for a Long,
Happy Life Together

11

Part II

Cat Training 101

67

Part III

Advanced Lessons in Cat Training

137

Acknowledgments

No book is produced by the author alone. I gratefully acknowledge the contributions of my wife, Izolda, cofounder of the World Famous Popovich Comedy Pet Theater; our daughter, Anastasia, a stalwart performer in the show and helper with our menagerie of pets; my writing helper and researcher, Michael Sion; my editor at St. Martin's Press, Rose Hilliard; and—of course—the cats and dogs, ferrets and mice, geese and doves that make Comedy Pet Theater the hit sensation it is.

Introduction

Since each of us is blessed with only one life,
why not live it with a cat?
—Robert Stearns

When I first laid eyes on a beautiful white longhair kitten in an animal shelter in Las Vegas, I never could have imagined what destiny lay in store for each of us . . .

I had gone to the shelter on the advice of a friend, who knew I wanted to find a pet to complete my new household. I had been hired to work as a juggler and clown in my own act on the Midway at the Circus Circus Hotel and Casino. I'd moved my wife, Izolda, and our young daughter, Anastasia, to Las Vegas. What better way to start our life together in our new city, to help us settle into our new home, than to add a little furry friend? But when I'd gone to a pet store to buy a cat, the price was so steep I couldn't afford it!

That's when my friend told me that in America, strays and unwanted pets are placed for adoption in "shelters." This was a concept foreign to my Ukrainian mind. *How very American,*

I thought. *This country of consumers has stores where you can buy animals for pets . . . but just in case you don't want the pets anymore, there also are places where you can dispose of them!* At the shelter, I passed by rows and rows of cages holding sullen or forlorn dogs and cats, some of them surely abandoned by previous owners. My heart swelled with pity. Then I caught my breath and stood still. In front of me, behind the cage wire, sat a cat of about a year old with magnificent white fur.

I was glad to rescue Snow (as we named her) from the shelter and a likely premature end. She turned out to be the perfect choice: We three Popoviches were delighted with how playful our kitty turned out to be. Snow kept us constantly entertained by stalking and pouncing on whatever little object moved within her line of sight. What's more—to our great amusement—she habitually chased her tail, like a puppy.

As I marveled at this silly quirk of our new family member, a lightbulb flashed in my showman's mind. While I was a world-champion juggler, I was but a novice clown, and less confident in that part of my act. What if I brought the energetic Snow on stage with me to use as a backup gag to get the audience laughing—just in case my clown shenanigans did not go over? My notion was to bring Snow on stage hidden in one of my bags. During my jester antics I'd reach for the bag, unfasten its top—and my frisky friend would leap out! She'd scamper about, pursuing her tail, and I'd clutch my head like a fool over having opened the wrong bag.

Well, not every show-biz idea works out. Fortunately for me, Snow's escapades proved to be a big winner. She cracked up the audience every time. The people who came to watch circus acts on the Midway loved the surprise of seeing this gorgeous little animal pop out from her bag and race around on stage. I didn't mind being upstaged at all. I was very proud of her. To my relief, Snow didn't mind the roar of people laughing and clapping, nor the blazing stage lights.

Frankly, the crowd's reaction should have been no surprise to me. Most of us have a soft spot in our hearts for cats and dogs. Before long, I fell under the spell of a much bolder idea . . .

AT THIS POINT I should tell you that I already was well accustomed to caring for pets, being a fourth-generation circus performer and the son of animal trainers. I was born in 1963 in the Soviet Union—in the city of Kiev, in what now is known only as the country of Ukraine. I grew up in the circus world. My mother and father, Alexei and Tamara, were jugglers and performers who worked with dogs on stage. Their act was a part of the Great Moscow Circus. From an early age, I was given tasks of feeding and looking after the dogs in my parents' act. I liked playing with the animals, but also knew that caring for them was a great responsibility. From close, intimate contact I learned to understand them as well as enjoy their company. Frankly, these dogs and I formed a tight bond, and I gained a respect for domestic animals that would last a lifetime.

At age 5 I began assisting my mother on stage with her trained dogs. The next year my father began teaching me the art of juggling, and at 12 I became a professional, performing with a small circus. By 14 I had my first solo act—juggling while balancing on a freestanding ladder. My father continued as my stalwart coach, and at age 16 I hit the big time: joining the Great Moscow Circus. I was very driven to succeed. My skills progressed through endless, rigorous rehearsing and performing, and I eventually became a key attraction in the Moscow circus and its representative in international competitions. I captured a number of prestigious juggling crowns. Craving new challenges, I also trained as an acrobat and clown, and completed a five-year course to earn a degree as a circus creator and producer. As a sideline, I appeared in a starring role in three Russian movies.

In 1991, I became the first person from the former Soviet Union to perform with the Ringling Bros. and Barnum & Bailey Circus. This meant moving to America and learning English. I burned to impress American audiences, and pushed myself very hard. In one stunt I balanced on a nine-foot-tall freestanding ladder while juggling nine rings—in the process, setting a world record. The next year my juggling act was hired by Circus Circus in Las Vegas, where my wife and I performed in a lineup of circus acts.

Well, Snow—as I've mentioned—proved to be a big hit in my clown routine, and so I quickly embarked on a much grander scheme for my show: creating a full-scale feature based around cat tricks. Now, I considered that training domestic cats would be extremely difficult, and perhaps even impossible, given their famously independent streak that knows no rival in the world of domestic animals. But that would be to my advantage, too, since no one else had thought of (or dared) to train housecats.

Soon I had adopted a few more cats from the shelter and set them up in comfort at my home. I'd chosen them for their outgoing personalities in the shelter, and their young ages. None was older than 1 year. Slowly I began rehearsing with them. As expected, this was no easy task. Patience quickly became my operative word. A domestic cat cannot be taught to do what it doesn't want to do. Some cats naturally like to

Felix and Pusha performing a trick.

jump; others are climbers; others still are prone to walking around their owner's legs. But a climber would not feel like playing a game of pouncing from one point to the next, just as a jumper wouldn't show any interest in shimmying up a pole just for a reward of kind words from its master.

I carefully studied each cat in turn for a lengthy period to understand its character. Then I set about playing with it. If it was a jumper (like Snow) prone to tracking and tackling a piece of yarn, that was our trick, and I slowly trained the cat to hop from one stool to another, then through a hoop. If the cat was a walker, I coaxed it to amble along a thin rope between two ladders. Ten minutes was the maximum of daily rehearsal per cat. And even ten minutes was too long for one session. I broke the sessions into five minutes each—played once in the morning, and once in the evening.

Once I'd found the right game for a cat, it took to it with great enjoyment. As the weeks went by I gradually increased the lighting and sound in the training room until the cat would feel comfortable performing on stage in front of an audience. After interminable rehearsals with each cat, I brought my newly organized cast of furry performers to Circus Circus in an act I christened, "Cat Skills."

Performing three times a day, six days a week, the cats proved their worthiness as entertainers. To be sure, there were times when I'd look into a cat's eyes and see it had no interest at that moment in responding to my cues. So be it! Even human performers display attitude from time to time. With a cat, though, there would be no use in attempting to change its mind at that moment and rousing it into action. And so I'd move on to another cat that was sitting on its perch, waiting for its turn to play a little game with its master. I had been in show business long enough to appreciate the necessity of backup plans. This is one reason why I brought multiple cats on stage. But the happy news was that most cats did respond on cue on stage. And the even happier news was that children of all ages—meaning adults, too—responded with delight to the animal antics.

I knew my "Cat Skills" act was on its way to being a hit.

AS WORD SPREAD ABOUT my show, I began attracting national media attention. I scored a feature article in *People* magazine. My cats and I appeared twice on *The Tonight Show*. In America, people generally are fond of their pets—and always eager to applaud them when they do wild or crazy stunts. And I offered stunts that truly were original. A cat pushing a dog in a baby carriage. A dog in a classroom solving a math problem and another erasing a chalkboard. (Yes, I eventually added dogs—also rescued from shelters—to my show.)

I took my act on tour around the world, settled for a time in Branson, Missouri, where I performed Comedy Pet Theater at the Magical Palace, and returned to Vegas in 2005. The next year I debuted The World Famous Popovich Comedy Pet Theater at the V Theater in the Aladdin Resort and Casino, on the Las Vegas Strip. The V Theater, in the Miracle Mile mall, now is part of Planet Hollywood Resort & Casino. My afternoon show plays there daily. I've added geese and doves, white mice and ferrets. The place usually is packed. And while all the troupe members—including my wife, daughter and I, and several clowns and acrobats—receive our fair share of applause, the cats seem to garner the loudest clapping and cheers.

Sometimes I get a feeling they relish this status.

ALTHOUGH I AM A professional entertainer and my pets work on stage, they are still pets, and treated as part of my family. All the animals in my trained menagerie are well cared for at the Popovich residence. They are loved and pampered. They are provided a comfortable environment, healthy food, playtime and toys, and regular veterinary checkups.

Even after all these years—meaning, my whole life—living or working with cats, I still treasure the moments of connection with these dear creatures that share my daily life. There is an ancient bond between humans and pets. It is undeniable that our species reaps much in the way of emotional rewards—joy and satisfaction, companionship and affection—in return for providing protection, sustenance, and comfort to our furry friends. They've certainly taught me more than I've taught them.

Because I have absorbed a great amount of knowledge about how to get along with cats, I finally felt compelled to

write the book you are reading now. In the following chapters I am sharing not only basic information that is vital knowledge for being a happy cat owner, but also insights I believe you will find nowhere else.

Like any family member, your pet cat can prove challenging to live with. You must establish rules to maintain a harmonious relationship. Fortunately, there are no problems without solutions. You can teach your cat not to claw the sofa—or you! You can train it not to rouse you from slumber. With practice, you can learn to communicate quite fluently with your cat.

In the chapters that follow, I will share with you the secrets I've learned about keeping both owner and cat happy. In Part I, I'll discuss the critical period of welcoming a new cat into the household and laying the groundwork for a strong, fulfilling relationship. In Part II, I'll discuss problems that may arise and training techniques to help maintain a healthy relationship with your cat. And in Part III, I'll offer more advanced cat-training secrets that I've learned from working so closely with cats for a great many years.

None of the lessons I share are difficult to absorb, and not all of them will apply to your particular situation. For example, if you don't move to a new home, you won't need to know how to help your cat adjust to strange new surroundings. Or perhaps you won't be traveling with your cat. Or intending to train it to do tricks.

Well, all I can say is that one never knows what the future holds! If there are chapters that don't seem relevant to you now, they eventually might be. I never would have predicted—upon seeing the little snow-white kitty in the Las Vegas animal shelter more than a dozen years ago—that I would develop a world-famous act built around housecats. Or be writing a book about the intricacies of cat ownership.

Snow—you brought more adventure into my life than I ever could have imagined!

Part I

Laying the Groundwork for a Long, Happy Life Together

1

The Connection
Between Humans and Cats

Thousands of years ago, cats were worshipped as gods.
Cats have never forgotten this.
—ANONYMOUS

The feline we know as the domestic cat or housecat has cohabitated with humans since long before the dawn of recorded time. Whatever it is that sustains the mutual attraction that first spurred this partnership, it has continued to this day. Perhaps the explanation is that humans and cats were made for each other.

There is evidence from a genetic study that the direct ancestors of today's domestic cats broke away from their wild counterparts and began living with humans more than 100,000 years ago. The study's coauthor, Stephen O'Brien, chief of the Laboratory of Genomic Diversity at the National Cancer

Institute in Frederick, Maryland, remarked about the housecat's special character. "The felidae family is well known as a successful predator—very deadly, very ferocious, very threatening to all species including humankind," he said. "But this little guy actually chose not to be that. He actually chose to be a little bit friendly and also was a very good mouser."

Good news for it. The bearlike saber-toothed tiger has been extinct for thousands of years. The clever little housecat is thriving. Estimates indicate there as many as 600 million of these creatures in the world today.

A question arises: Who made the first move in the bonding between cat and human? What drew this curious sub-species of feline toward the fires and shelters of human settlements?

Knowing the independent nature of cats, it is likely that they initially sought out the company of humans, not vice versa. And what, exactly, did these upright, two-legged, rather naked creatures have to offer their much smaller, four-legged and furry, fellow mammals?

The explanation is simple: farms. Early agricultural settlements were infested by rodents attracted by grain stores. The mice and other vermin, in turn, attracted cats. And the cats—being lethal hunters—garnered the gratitude of the farmers. The partnership deal likely was sealed by the cats' openness to establishing permanent residence in the farming communities, partaking of shelter and food offered by human settlers in return for their mouser duties. But we shouldn't ignore two other appealing qualities: the relative ease in caring for pet cats, and cats' affectionate manner toward their human providers.

. . .

ONCE THE DOMESTIC CAT had made its move to live along-
side humans, it has been this unique animal's fate to have
been venerated as well as vilified, depending on the period of
history.

In Egyptian civilization, founded on the grain harvest, the
cat gained godlike stature. Many Egyptians owned cats, and
when a pet cat died, families customarily shaved their eyebrows in mourning. Cats were mummified and buried in
special cemeteries. Killing a cat was a capital offense, even if
done accidentally. The sight of a dead cat could cause people
to flee from the scene—fearing they'd be implicated in the
crime. Egyptians were so fond and jealous of their cats that
they sent missions to neighboring lands to buy cats that had
been illegally exported. But such programs could not contain
the popularity of cats inside any one nation's border; the animal's usefulness in catching rodents, as well as cats' suitabil-
ity as pets, guaranteed their eventual spread around the
globe.

The Romans, conquerors of Egypt and much of northern
Africa, southwest Asia, and Europe, discovered that cats were
more effective at controlling vermin than the ferrets the empire builders had been using. And so the Romans introduced
cats throughout their expanding realm. Sailors and traders
found cats to be perfect for controlling populations of rats on
ships—and so cats traveled the oceans and seas to more distant lands.

As in Egypt, cats gained status in many religions. But that
proved a liability to this popular pet as Christianity took
hold in the Roman Empire. Church officials wanted to abol-
ish paganism. Their efforts made cats a target for a crusade
to change people's perceptions about these widely worshipped
animals. By the middle ages, the popular perception of cats

had shifted from veneration to vilification; common folk considered cats to be cunning creatures, and associated them with witchcraft. Strays were hunted and killed under the belief that they could be used in pagan rites, or even be witches in disguise. The lingering superstition that a black cat brings bad luck stems from this medieval belief. In some locales, the killing of a cat became part of an official public holiday program, to symbolize the banishment of the devil.

Throughout the ages, cats have proved useful to humans in numerous ways—including as mousers, companions, and even objects of religious devotion. They also have been targets of superstition.

A woman, full of anxiety, approached a well-known dermatologist and asked, "Doctor, is it true that you can make warts disappear forever by burying a black cat in a cemetery under a full moon?"

"Hmm," said the doctor, adopting a pensive look, chin in hand. "Well, yes. This result would be a certainty—providing the warts were on the cat."

Fortunately, such inhumane cruelty is rare in modern times. Today, cats' age-old function as mouse hunters continues in agriculture. Researchers have calculated that in one year, one mouse-hunting cat can save ten tons of grain from mice. Science may have no better substitute as a controller of vermin. But cats' usefulness to humans has extended beyond being rodent killers. Some people ardently believe that cats are psychic.

Reports have come from around the globe of cats predicting natural disasters. For example, officials ordered the evacuation of Haicheng, China, in February 1975 following reports not only of seismic activity but peculiarly anxious behavior of cats and other animals. A magnitude 7.3 temblor struck a few days after the evacuation of the city of 1 million. Stories have been recorded of cats hiding or trying to escape the house, or of mother cats dragging their kittens to safer spots, before humans were aware of impending storms, floods, or volcanic eruptions. A legend from World War II (never confirmed by scientific study, as wartime resources were needed elsewhere) holds that cats could predict air raids by their fur standing on end before a siren wailed.

But scientific explanations surely can be discovered for why cats may be able to sense incoming aircrafts, earthquakes, or thunderstorms before their human masters know what's coming. In relation to sirens, perhaps cats hear distant sound waves or feel vibrations before we humans do. As for storms, electrical discharges in the atmosphere can send electromagnetic waves that saturate the air with positive ions, and which can act on chemical substances in the brain. (Some people suffer headaches during these periods.) Cats may be more sensitive than we are to these ions. Similarly, cats may be more attuned to gases that emanate from a volcano before it erupts. As for detecting earthquakes, cat paws are very sensitive, and perhaps can feel very slight earth tremors as they build.

Whether cats are more sensitive to environmental cues— or actually are prescient—the fact remains they often seem able to sense coming disasters before we humans can.

· · ·

ONE PARTICULAR ROLE in which housecats excel is in their companionship with their human masters—providing their owners sheer comfort and pleasure just by coexisting with them. One possible explanation is that humans are hardwired for parenting, and relate to pet animals as helpless children, tapping into the emotional fulfillment that comes from parenting. Pets also are known to lower their owners' blood pressure. My late mother, who was plagued by hypertension in her latter years, told me that when her cat curled at her feet, her stress dropped and she felt deep relaxation.

Dr. James Serpell, director of the Center for the Interaction of Animals and Society, at the University of Pennsylvania, has written that keeping a pet reduces the number of the owner's visits to the doctor, lengthens survival following a heart attack, and wards off depression.

IT IS OBVIOUS TO ME that the ancient bond between cats and humans will continue for the rest of civilization. As founder of the World Famous Popovich Comedy Pet Theater, I have a closer relationship with cats than do most people. My silent communication with cats has allowed me to train them to perform consistently on stage. My connection with cats is very well developed, and I credit this skill to my careful tuning in to these animals' abilities to understand us, and to perceive their environment. Most people are unaware of just how sensitive cats are. I myself continue to be astonished by my own cats' intelligence and sensitivity from time to time.

In fact, I've even come to suspect that an intelligent cat can read its owner's thoughts. One day I was working at my computer at the kitchen table, and decided I would skip lunch and continue typing away. I uttered nary a word about this decision. Within seconds, my cat Martin—a small but feisty gray mix—appeared at my feet. I realized he was begging for a piece of cheese from the refrigerator—whose door I had resolved not to open. I'd occasionally given him this sort of treat at luncthime. Sure enough, Martin ran to the fridge the moment I stood up, as if he were expecting the tasty morsel (which he readily received and devoured).

Yes, Martin is keenly perceptive. Another example: He hates riding in the car. Whenever my wife, daughter and I prepare to leave the house for a ride and decide to take Martin, he foresees this and disappears—usually under a bed. What is especially odd is that we began using code words about leaving, to avoid alerting him. We even used Russian and French, but the result was the same. Perhaps Martin understands not only simple human speech but its undertones? Or—as I've proposed is possible—could he actually read minds?

I've heard countless similar stories from friends. One has claimed that his tomcat can divine his mood even before my friend enters the house. If my friend is in a happy mood, the tomcat will meet him in the hall. If my friend is in a foul humor, his cat is nowhere to be found the moment his master steps inside the door.

Is this telepathy? One thing I know for sure is that cats possess powers of perception that demand serious scientific study. Another thing I know is that the strangeness and uniqueness of cats have endeared them to humankind since the beginning of our inter-species friendship, all those millennia ago.

The mysteriousness inherent in these wonderful creatures may go a long way toward explaining our love for them.

A "Purr-pourri" of Random Cat Trivia

• Cats have keener senses of smell than dogs. In the British Army, during World War I, cats were used for early detection of poison-gas attacks in the trenches. On submarines, cats were used to detect gas leaks.

• European shorthaired cats are considered the best defenders of grain against rats and the mice.

• Cats share a trait with giraffes and camels: They are the only animals that walk first with their left feet, then their right feet.

• Cats greatly love fresh air; therefore a window in the house should always be kept open, if possible.

• Cats sleep approximately 18 hours a day. Newspapers, with their soft, warm texture, are one preferred surface for cats.

• If a cat seems finicky about its food—sniffing it then turning away—consider how long the food has sat in a bowl. A cat's nose performs the role of thermometer.

• The darkness of the spots on a Siamese cat's fur depends on the climate in which it lives. In colder regions, the spots are darker. Siamese kittens are born with all-white fur, since the temperature in the womb keeps the spots from growing dark.

• A Japanese magazine featured the photograph of a tomcat that had traveled 100 kilometers to return to its masters, with whom he had lived since he was a kitten. After several years, a daughter in the family took the cat with her when she moved to a new home. But the cat disappeared the very day of his arrival at the new place. A year later, he showed up at his old home, filthy, bedraggled, and having lost a kilogram of weight.

 • Cats can succumb to many illnesses that plague humans, including diabetes, pleurisy, cancer, stomach ulcers, and obesity.

• Stress is a known contributor to a number of diseases, and one treatment for lowering stress levels in patients is acquiring a pet cat. Doctors in the United States have prescribed this remedy.

• Scientists have found that cradling a cat can lower a person's blood pressure, and temper an angry mood.

• Cat lovers may find this shocking, but some people are afraid of cats. This isn't necessarily because of superstition (such as the medieval association of cats with witchcraft and the devil), but because these people suffer from a documented psychological condition: ailurophobia. They may fear getting scratched or bitten, and may break out in sweat, grow short of breath, or even grow hysterical at the sight of a cat.

• Those familiar with cats know that when a person consciously tries to ignore a cat, the cat is prone to approach and even climb up on the poor soul. Famous sufferers of ailurophobia even include two men celebrated as great warriors: Julius Caesar and Napoleon Bonaparte.

2

Choosing Your Cat: How, Where, Why

*"One small cat changes coming home
to an empty house to coming home."*
—Pam Brown

So you're considering getting a cat. This will be a big change for your household—but an even bigger change for the cat. If, after deciding to bring a cat into your family, you decide it wasn't a good idea, you can bid it good-bye by finding it another home, and life for you will resume as normal. But for the poor animal, the uprooting will be devastating.

Therefore, consider your situation carefully before deciding to get a cat. Discuss the issue with the other members of your household. Is anyone allergic to cats? (Having everyone who lives in your home spend time at a friend's home where there are cats can reveal this.) Is anyone uncomfortable with or hostile toward cats? Who will be the main caretaker—ultimately in charge of feeding it, cleaning its litter box, and taking it to the veterinarian? (If there is a pregnant woman in the house, consider that she will not be cleaning the litter box. This point, about avoiding toxoplasmosis, will be discussed in Chapter Thirteen.) Can your household budget afford these expenses? Who will let it in and out if you decide it will be an indoor-outdoor cat? Is there a pet door already in the home? Where will the cat sleep?

Another consideration is whether to get a cat or a kitten. If there is a small child in the house, at an age where, out of curiosity, the child could harm a defenseless kitten by pulling its tail or otherwise abusing it, a cat is a better choice. But if there's already an adult cat in the house, a kitten might be better. If you bring in another adult cat, each is set in its habits, and jealousy is bound to flare. Usually, a kitten will get along with its fellow animals, as long as they are correctly acquainted. (This will be discussed further in Chapter Fourteen.)

If you don't have enough time and patience to raise a kitten, you can acquire an adult cat that won't wear you out with its hyper energy. But most people prefer getting a kitten, raising it from the start, and enjoying its cuteness and playfulness. Just make sure you realize that kittens are full of energy and the urge to explore, just like human children. Freestanding breakable objects such as vases that can easily be knocked over by a frisky kitty should be removed to safer areas. Your cat will want to sharpen its claws, so a scratching post or multiple scratching posts are a wise addition. Also know that some household plants are toxic to cats. These include Easter lily and oleander. Your veterinarian can provide a more complete list.

The optimal age for a kitten to be adopted is 10 to 12

weeks. A quick check by you is in order, to ensure it has a complete set of teeth. The kitten must have reached the development stage at which it has been weaned and is able to eat solid food. It will have learned from its mother the basics of cat knowledge, such as eating, washing, and the play motions it will need in case of a fight or a hunt (lying in expectation, pouncing, and grumbling over its caught prey). By this age, the kitten should have received its first vet exam and vaccinations, and been "wormed"—meaning, received medications to combat intestinal parasites.

When the kitten is old enough to be adopted, it will have built up its immunities and strength to handle moving to a new home. Mentally, it now is ready to bond with a new owner. However, if it has had little contact with people up to this point, it may be predisposed to flight. When choosing a kitten, it's best to get one "raised underfoot"—accustomed to humans and their everyday household noises. However, if you treat a skittish kitten with love and patience, it will eventually accept you as its trusted master.

When I screen a kitten before choosing it to take home, I check for bright eyes, sparkling energy, and playfulness. I make sure it has clean ears, eyes, and nose, and clean fur with no evidence of diarrhea. I see that it is of normal physical size. I want a kitty that is already healthy and happy.

WHERE TO GO TO get a cat?

If you are looking for a purebred cat to exhibit, you must contact a reputable breeder in your area. I discourage you from buying a purebred from a pet store, where the supplier may be dubious. Sometimes you can find breeders through newspaper advertisements, but a better starting place is scanning the listings section of a cat magazine, or surfing the Internet, or attending a cat show. At the show, chat with exhibitors and get referrals to breeders.

Visiting the breeder's cattery is vital; check out the environment, which can affect a cat's temperament and health. Make sure the premises are sanitary. Ensure the food and water supplies are clean, the litter boxes tended to, the adult toms separated from the rest of the cats. It is preferable that the kittens are being raised in the house around people, since they grow accustomed to people sounds such as vacuum cleaners and doorbells and won't panic from such noises in your house.

My favorite source for acquiring a cat is a local animal shelter. It rescues the animal from a probable fate of being destroyed—as are tens of thousands of unwanted cats every year. Many if not most of these misfortunate animals are healthy and would have made perfect pets. They become aban-

To Fix or Not to Fix?

Unless you are a cat breeder by profession or as a serious cat fancier, you have no valid reason not to have your cat fixed. A fertile female cat can by itself account for about 10 kittens in its first year, and more than 50 over six years. The best argument for sterilization is that millions of unwanted domestic cats are euthanized every year. Cats can be surgically sterilized as early as six to eight weeks, and it's better to have them fixed prior to puberty.

doned for a variety of reasons. Many end up in a shelter as the product of unwanted litters, due to cat owners who neglect to sterilize their pets. Some cats are sent to shelters for reasons that are utterly contemptible, such as an owner losing interest in the animal.

I have scrutinized the eyes of onetime pets that were shabbily discarded by their owners, ending up in shelter cages. Some stare with incomprehension, confused about why they have been stuck in a strange, tiny confined space. The reality of their predicament hasn't sunk in yet. Others seem to be wrestling with a big question: *Why did my master reject me?* Then there are those who look like they are marking time, resigned to their fate—knowing a passing human will not claim it. But there also are those that respond enthusiastically when you stop at their cage—eager to be liberated by a new master.

I can say from experience that, if you're not seeking a

Future members of Gregory's family.

purebred, you have a very good chance of finding the right cat for yourself at a shelter. And you can rest assured that the animal will be grateful to you for taking it home.

Keep in mind that adopting a shelter cat will require some patience and sympathy. When a cat loses its master, or a kitten is taken from its mother, it loses not only its caretaker but also its home in which it feels comfortable and familiar. In other words, it loses nearly everything dear to it. It is removed to a cage in a strange and rather forbidding shelter. The poor animal ceases to be oriented in its space, and feels as if it has lost part of itself. In this sense it is worse off than a cat born out on the street or in an abandoned building.

Over time—perhaps a few days, perhaps a few weeks— you will gain the cat's trust. It will adapt to its new surroundings, recognize you as its new and faithful provider, and accept your home as its home.

HERE'S ONE MORE DECISION you may not have anticipated at the start of your search:

Should you get one cat, or two?

Often, two cats is the wise solution, for the pair will keep each other company, especially during your absence.

My wife, daughter and I wrestled with this decision when we looked for a kitten as a simple housepet (as opposed to training it for my stage show). We considered that if we took home one kitten, it would grow more strongly attached to us. If we took two, they would keep each other occupied, but might end up ignoring us.

Well, we finally settled on taking just one. But two years later we saw the need to add a second pet cat. We found that we couldn't devote sufficient time to caressing and playing with the first cat, even though we loved her dearly and provided for all her needs. In hindsight, I wish we'd gotten two right at the start. As I write this, the two-year-old cat, named Martina, is getting used to the kitten, Francesca.

If you are living on your own and spend many hours a day outside your home, it's better to have a pair of cats than to leave one home alone, lonely and bored.

When you are considering getting two cats, you very well may spot two kittens that already are bonded with each other, playing or sleeping together, hanging out somewhat apart from the others. They are a match. If you're leaning toward taking both, it's best to take them at the same time. It will ease the transition into the new household.

THERE ARE TIMES WHEN a cat chooses *you,* instead of you choosing it. A few cats in my World Famous Popovich Comedy Pet Theater came to me this way.

It is painful for me to visit an animal shelter, knowing that I can't take home every little animal whose cage I pass and which makes a quick, silent connection with me. Because I am very attuned to animals, it's like I can read these wards' thoughts. Some are extremely anxious about their fate, and wish to be removed from their cage to a better place. My backyard has facilities to house more animals in the space and comfort they need, but my resources are limited. On the rare occasion when I do visit a shelter these days, knowing I have room to accommodate another healthy and outgoing animal whose life would be prematurely cut short if not adopted in the next few weeks, I must be very selective. In my pool of performers are cats of different breeds or mixes. I want to find a healthy young cat that will add to the diversity.

I force myself to resist looking too closely at every cute creature in its cage. I try to ignore them as I focus on finding the right candidate to add to my troupe.

But there have been times when a cat meets my eyes and continues following me with its gaze even as I leave the room. When I return and pass its cage, the cat connects with me again. Some sparks fly between us. I may already have settled on a different cat, but the pull of attraction from this one leads me to ask a shelter worker to bring this cat out of its cage. I watch how it behaves in the worker's arms. I ask myself, *Does it like people? Is it alert and energetic? Is it still interested in me?* I'll observe from a distance. The cat continues paying attention to me—silently communicating that we have some chemistry—and I entertain the thought of giving it a home.

I return to canvassing the cages in the shelter. But finally, resigned, I walk up to the cat's cage and say, "Look, you better come with me."

Some people similarly find themselves chosen by strays, whose loitering and attention encourage them to put out food. If you're considering taking in a stray, make sure you take it to a vet since it may have picked up any number of parasites and diseases.

And please make sure the cat doesn't belong to someone else. If there is no collar, bring the cat to a veterinarian or shelter and have the animal scanned to see whether it has a microchip ID that will help you reunite it with its owner. Or you might ask your neighbors if they know who the cat belongs to.

If the owner cannot be found . . . well, then you can claim the cat as your own. Perhaps it already has claimed *you*.

Some people are superstitious and believe that a cat that

appears out of nowhere and becomes a regular presence at their home is a reincarnated being that, perhaps, used to live at the home. I don't make light of such a belief, and if it works for superstitious people, fine. My own theory is that an animal can feel the aura of a home. If it's a residence with a lot of hostility and tension among its occupants, then the cat will be repelled and not choose to hang out there. But if it's a residence that is essentially pleasant, this will compel a cat to seek to join the fold. And if the people of the home graciously provide the cat food and a welcoming spirit—well, then they've passed the cat's test.

In the part of the world I come from—the Slavic countries— cats are venerated as symbols of a harmonious household. A folk custom when a family moves into a new home is to have a cat walk first across the threshold into the home, to rid the place of any bad spirits and to bring good luck. In fact, a cat is considered essential to making a family complete. The cat symbolizes the family's kindness and closeness. A dog may protect a home with its watchfulness and strength, but a cat protects the home from disharmony.

🐾 PAW PRINTS 🐾

- Avoid getting a small kitten if there is a small child in the house who could unintentionally harm the defenseless animal.
- A kitten should be adopted between ages 10 to 12 weeks, after it has been weaned. Check that its mouth has a full set of teeth.
- If you wish to exhibit your cat, you must acquire it from a reputable breeder. Visit the cattery to ensure it is a clean environment.
- Screen a kitten before taking it home. Check for bright eyes, sparkling energy, healthy size, playfulness, and clean ears, eyes, nose, and fur.
- If no one in the home will have sufficient time to play with the kitten, consider getting two. Seek kittens already bonded with each other. Bring them home at the same time to ease the transition.
- A cat adopted from a shelter can initially react with suspicion. Be patient, and it will grow accustomed to you.

3

The Cat's First Days
in Your Home

"I love cats because I love my home,
and after awhile they become its visible soul."
—Jean Cocteau

Now that you've chosen a cat, its first days in your home will be an adjustment for it as well as you. If it is a kitten, after bringing it home you must place it in a warm, secluded area. Try not to fuss too much over it, but avoid the other extreme of abandoning it or leaving it to its own mischief. Keep an eye on it, but don't smother your new pet.

If you brought the cat home in a carrier, place the carrier on the floor and leave the door open so that the cat can come out on its own and begin inspecting its new territory. The cat may end up returning to sleep in the cage, or select another safe spot, such as under a bed or couch. Next to the carrier place the water bowl and the food bowl, and the litter box.

To ease its transition, feed it with the same food it has been eating, and add to its litter box some of the newspaper or litter from its previous box. It will recognize the smells and feel a sense of familiarity. As the days pass, you can gradually shift to the food and litter you prefer. (Know that for the first few days, the cat, still anxious about its relocation, may not have much of an appetite.)

It is essential to confine the cat to one room for the first few days, and then allow it to explore the home. Even an adult cat must be kept inside for about two weeks—to prevent it from running off, and to impress upon it the sense of its new home. If you have young children in the home, explain to them that the cat will be kept apart from the family until it has adjusted to its new residence. The children will want to hold the cat, and you can permit this, but under supervision and only for a brief period.

Overall, you must be prepared to devote extra time and attention to your family's new addition. In fact, you must prepare before its arrival to make your home hospitable and danger proof.

A checklist of supplies:

- Cat food. A quality brand of dry food has sufficient nutrition; wet food generally should be given sparingly, mixed in with the dry food.
- Food and water bowls.
- Cat bed. This can be a box or basket with a blanket in it. The animal will frequently ignore this arranged bed and select for itself a spot in the home to snooze. But especially in the early days, when the cat is confined to a room, it will have this bed at its disposal.

- Carrying container. This can be a cardboard box with a handle and air holes, available from a pet supplier.
- Scratching post. This is obtainable from a pet supplier.
- A beach chair (sold at pet stores) or other comfortable seat that will be placed in a quiet, secluded area of the home as the cat's refuge. (More on this later in the chapter.)
- Several cat toys. These can include a stuffed mouse, a feather, or a paper butterfly on a stick.

It also is necessary to make your home safe for the new occupant. Cats, and especially kittens, are extremely curious and inquisitive. They will be spending a great deal of time unsupervised, roaming about. You can make your cat's explorations less risky to its health by adopting the following precautions:

- Reposition loose electrical cords to where a cat can't get at them with its teeth. If this is not possible, cover the cords with special shielding tubes. (One brand is Critter-Cord.)
- Tie curtains or shades tighter so they don't move. Curtains swaying from a breeze trigger a cat's hunting instinct to paw and pounce.
- Don't allow your cat to get into the habit of jumping on the stove. One day the burner will be on and the cat will scorch its paws.
- Cats love leaping onto and navigating elevated surfaces. Therefore, do not leave breakable dishes, glasses, or sharp knives or forks on the kitchen or dining-room table.
- Remove vases and other small breakable objects from windowsills, accessible shelves, and table edges.

- Don't leave small objects lying around on which the kitten can choke or injure itself, such as buttons, needles, or rubber bands.
- Cover trash cans so tasty smells don't tempt the cat to rummage inside.
- Place a screen in front of a warm fireplace to prevent an inexperienced kitten from getting singed or charred.
- Make sure drawers and appliances, such as refrigerators, are shut. Kittens, especially, can crawl inside and get trapped.
- Always check the dishwasher, washing machine, or dryer before starting it up, to ensure the cat isn't inside.
- Keep the toilet seat lid down to prevent a cat falling in.
- When you go to sit on the sofa or in an armchair, make sure there isn't a warm little body already curled up where you are about to lower your weight.

The preceding recommendations should quickly become second nature to you. They are especially important to heed during the first few weeks, when a cat is becoming acquainted with its new surroundings and forming its habits.

Like children, cats love to explore, and they discover the world around them through all five senses. Your task is to allow them to learn their environment without suppressing their healthy curiosity, while taking precautions to make their journeys as safe as possible.

IT WILL BE DIFFICULT for you to temporarily keep your new pet isolated in its own area, behind a closed door, but it's the wise choice to help it become oriented to its new surroundings. It should get acquainted with the rest of the family, including pets, gradually. After a few days, you may permit it to roam the home at large.

To establish a positive relationship from the start, always speak to the cat in a calm and friendly tone, and do not speak loudly to it. One of the first signs of its acceptance of you as a friend, not a foe, will be its positive response to your voice. If it is hiding as you enter its area, it may peek out at you.

Don't be alarmed if the cat, for the first few days, remains hidden under a sofa or bed, or cowers in its cage, avoiding you. It may even mew loudly, expressing panic, especially on the first day. This is its natural reaction to its change in situation, and its fear of being alone. A kitten, especially, will exhibit this behavior. Your best response is to take it in your hands, stroke it gently, and speak to it in a comforting voice. The kitten will respond to the warmth and grow calm.

In any event, you continue cleaning its litter box, changing its water regularly, and keeping its food bowl filled. You also must talk to your cat. In good time, perhaps after a few days, the cat will understand that you aren't a danger to it. You should not be in a hurry to tame it until it has adjusted to its new home.

Name your cat as early as possible—perhaps even on its first day in your home. To encourage your cat to respond to its name, I suggest keeping the name short (one or two syllables, possibly three) and easily pronounced—something a cat can quickly hear and recognize from a distance. It must be a name with hard or stressed consonants—resonating. Something like "Hugh" or "Lola" won't do; but "Huey" or "Lolita," "Rascal" or "Kiki" will. "Alex" is better, because it has two consonants that command attention. "Sunny" is fine; the sibilance will get the cat to perk up its ears, and the "n" is sufficiently distinct. Cats also seem to respond to names that end with the "ee" sound.

It's important that the name mean something to the owner, that it relates to the owner's affection for the cat. Thus, the sound of the name will be expressive when you call it out. The cat will sense this warmth. An all-black kitty that looks a bit spooky can be called "Spooky," or "Spider," perhaps. A kitten that is very ingratiating can be christened "Player." A kitten that proves itself a very quick learner may be dubbed "Einstein."

You will know you've chosen the right name when it seems to perfectly fit the animal. It will almost seem like the name was predestined.

There's another nuance to this issue, although it's not scientific. I believe that a name can influence the animal's personality. Perhaps this is because the cat will be treated in a way that encourages it to fulfill its name. "Princess" may receive extra pampering; "Bruno" may be expected to be more physical, and thus be given the opportunity to play harder, or roam outside longer. "Arthur"? He's allowed to be more of a lazy sloth, an indoor-only cat.

When calling the cat by its name, enunciate the name as distinctly as you would if addressing a human, to distinguish the name as not being just another word. If the cat responds to its name, reward it with strokes and kind words of encouragement. Be patient. A cat should recognize its name after four or six weeks. After five or six months, a cat properly trained to answer to its name will come when you call it even from afar. (If you happen to adopt a cat that knew a previous name for itself, the process of accepting and reacting to its new name may take a bit longer.) And remember that when scolding your cat, never scold it by name or you're encouraging your cat to ignore you when you address it by name. A strong "no" or "bad cat" will be much more effective.

AFTER THE CAT HAS SETTLED into its new home, it will crave interaction with its human masters. This is especially true of kittens. It will play madly with toys, or with you wielding a toy. Keep in mind that a cat's play activity generally occurs in the evening.

You will decide early on whether you want your cat to be an indoor cat exclusively, or whether you'll allow it to roam outside. Indoor cats, on average, live much longer than cats exposed to such perils as automobile traffic, dogs, and other cats from which it can get a disease. If you do decide to let your cat go outside, establish one specific entrance and exit point for it, such as a pet door with a flap. The cat will develop a mental map of its routes, and you will be better able to monitor its comings and goings. Guard against the cat using other exits, such as the front door.

Provide your cat with a beach chair or some other comfortable seat, which should be placed in a secluded area of the home as a place where the cat can retreat and not be bothered when it needs some space. This is its private haven in which it must not be disturbed. The only exceptions are if it has hidden there at bath time, or if there is an emergency. Otherwise, grant the cat its special space.

Your cat's territory and independence will develop as it grows. By the age of three months, a kitten may be very eager to explore outside. Again, until it is fully grown, about six months old, you must keep a close eye on it if you permit it to go outside.

As a kitten accepts its role as the family pet, it will begin following you around. After all, it seeks a mentor to imitate, and you are serving the role of elder cat. (If an older cat already resides in your home, it may fill this purpose.) If you're eating at the kitchen table, the kitten will want to join you. The same with sleeping with you on your bed, whether it's welcome there or not.

There are sound methods of breaking these bad habits, and they will be discussed in Part II: Cat Training 101.

Zuzu.

🐾 PAW PRINTS 🐾

- To ease a cat's acclimation to its new home, for the first few days give it the same cat food it had been eating at its previous home, and incorporate the same newspaper or litter from its old box into its new box.

A Dozen Cat Myths Declawed

Certain notions about cats and their care have become deeply ingrained in our culture as well as in cultures around the world. But popular wisdom is not always rooted in reality. Here are some facts to counter misconceptions about our feline friends.

No. 1: A cat should have a saucer of milk each day.

After bringing home a strange cat, it's common for a person to fill a saucer of milk for the visitor. The truth is, milk contains few vitamins or minerals needed by the cat—such as iron and taurine. What's more, some cats are lactose intolerant and can get diarrhea. Even if a cat becomes accustomed to milk, you must remember that it is not a drink, but a source of additional nourishment. There is no substitute for fresh water, which must be continuously supplied in its water bowl. If a cat receives a sufficiently nutritious diet, milk is not necessary.

No. 2: Fish is a necessary staple for cats.

Popular cat-food brands often list fish in their ingredients. While cats like the taste, it isn't necessary to maintain their health. While fish contains taurine and Vitamin A, so do meat products.

The safest fish for a cat to eat is that contained in regular cat food. Avoid feeding a cat canned tuna or other fish meant for humans.

No. 3: Before being spayed, a female cat should be allowed to bear at least once, for its health.

Delayed sterilization heightens the risk of a cat developing

(Continued)

 diseases of the reproductive organs and mammary glands. The optimal age for spaying a cat is 5 to 6 months.

No. 4: After neutering, a tomcat becomes fat and lazy.

Actually, it becomes faster, calmer and more reasonable. Its lack of aggressiveness may make its owner see it as lazy. A tomcat's natural sleeping habit—of not less than 18 hours a day—can be mistaken for sloth.

No. 5: Cats heal their own wounds by licking them.

A cat's licking disinfects scratches or small wounds and contributes to healing, but if a wound is extensive, licking can deepen it. A cat's tongue is as rough as an emery board and can strip away upper layers of skin. An owner may need to place a sweater over the cat to cover the wound, or use a cone-shaped Elizabethan collar, also called a space collar, around the cat's neck to keep it from reaching the wound with its tongue.

No. 6: A cat always lands safely on its feet.

Cats are outstanding natural acrobats, with an instinct that helps them to land on their paws. When falling, a cat automatically turns its head and front paws, and its tail helps it control its airborne body, positioning all four paws toward the ground. But in truth, its belly impacts the ground as it lands. And a very long fall will lead to bone fractures, internal injuries and possibly death.

No. 7: Cats see as well in the dark as in daylight.

A cat's night vision is only a little better than a human's. Cats are natural-born hunters, and a cat's sensory advantage actually is its hearing. Another advantage is its sense of feeling from its whiskers—under its nose, on its eyebrows, and on its paws. Whiskers help the cat identify the position of an object.

As for daytime vision, domestic cats suffer from longsightedness, unable to clearly see objects right under their noses. They find a bowl of food by its smell. And their main interest when nuzzling food in the bowl is not the meal's taste, but its temperature.

No. 8: Whiskers help cats maintain their equilibrium.
A cat's whiskers are organs of touch, and have no relation at all to equilibrium.

No. 9: Cats and dogs are natural enemies.
Cats and dogs speak different languages, and frequently misunderstand or completely fail to understand each other. But that doesn't automatically make them foes. Contributing to the myth are tangles or chases caused by individual animals that are especially aggressive, or dogs with a hunting instinct prone to pursue any animal. But pets within a family, including cats and dogs, typically get along well.

No. 10: Siamese cats are aggressive.
Siamese cats are no more aggressive than other breeds. An individual Siamese can become aggressive due to brutal treatment by its owner, but this is true of all breeds. Siamese are, however, very spirited and more expressive of their emotions. Their voices are loud—although they are not the loudest of cats. That title is held by a hairless breed, sphynxes, which roar.

(Continued)

No. 11: Cats are insidious, and behave badly to spite their masters.

Behavioral problems in cats are usually connected to stress. Cats are very sensitive to their owners' moods and actions. A family quarrel or an owner's indifference to the cat can cause anxiety and depression, leading it to sulk or scratch furniture, or relieve itself outside its litter box. Some diseases, such as of the kidneys, can cause this, too.

I'll address one more myth on my own terms:

No. 12: Cats are people, only in cat bodies.

Science refutes this. But cats' humanlike behavior is confirmed by the daily experiences of cat owners.

- Keep a cat isolated from the rest of the home and contained behind a door for a few days, until it has adjusted to its surroundings and won't be tempted to flee.
- Safety proof your house for a cat, especially a kitten.
- Speak to your cat in a calm, friendly tone.
- Name your cat as early as possible, and choose a name that is short and easily pronounced, which a cat can recognize. Reward a cat with kind words and strokes every time it responds to its name. Don't scold your cat by name.
- If you decide to let your cat be an outdoor cat, establish one entrance/exit point. A pet door with a flap is ideal.

4

Mealtime:
What to Feed Your Cat

> *"I'm hungry. Therefore I am."*
> —GARFIELD, THE CARTOON CAT

Your cat should be given a regular feeding schedule that is adhered to religiously. This will help maintain its healthy diet—so it is not overfed or underfed—and also train it to show up punctually for the evening meal. And most importantly, it will discourage your cat from begging before its mealtime.

A cat usually consumes between 125 and 250 grams of food per day, and sometimes up to 300 grams. Kittens eat more frequently than adult cats. From three to six months of age, a kitten eats about six times a day; by eight months it falls into the routine of an adult cat, eating twice a day. Optimal feeding times correspond to the cat's periods of increased activity: once in the morning upon waking, and again at about six or seven o'clock at night.

What to feed your cat? Well, keep in mind that cats, like people, are highly individualistic. Some cats are finicky; others prefer several forms of food. Some stick purely with cat food; others appreciate a morsel of human food. One thing to keep in mind is that although a cat is domesticated, it nevertheless is a carnivorous predator by nature. Its diet in the wilds would be about 30 percent protein, so you should never attempt to put a cat on a vegetarian diet.

The nutrients it needs are found in quality dry cat food. As with all products, there are different grades of cat food. The least expensive brands typically contain numerous additives to boost taste and color, but are composed of meat byproducts such as bones, feathers, and skin. Their main ingredients are corn and wheat, soy, yeast and glutens. Like junk food for humans, cheap cat food is designed to taste good to a cat. But I don't find that cheap brands provide proper nutrition. Cats do not need carbohydrates.

The medium-priced brands contain fewer of the additives and the cheap grains that are contained in the low-cost brands. Medium-cost brands also contain vitamins, minerals, and oils to prevent ailments such as hairballs. These brands contain meat byproducts of a higher grade than the cheaper brands.

The premium brands are my preference. They don't contain taste- and color-boosting additives, and they are made of quality meat and grains, such as rice. These brands offer all the nutrition your cat needs.

Animal experts constantly are in disagreement over what constitutes an ideal diet for a domestic cat. Some swear by

Sebastian, Sugar, Zuzu, and Orange.

top-grade canned cat food, arguing that it has less carbohydrates than wet food. Others favor dry food, arguing that it's better for the cat's dental health than dry food. Ultimately, the choice is up to you—and your cat.

If you're thinking about sharing your own food with your pet, keep in mind that some breeds can suffer greatly from the seasonings and spices found in prepared human food. In no instance does a cat benefit from specially cooked foods from its human master. Consider that cats have cohabited

 A tomcat saunters into a neighborhood pub in New York City, jumps up on the bar and in perfect English says, "Gimme a double shot of bourbon."

The bartender, shocked, hurries over to the pub's owner, who's sitting at a back table, reading the newspaper. "Listen," the bartender says, "that tomcat just showed up and ordered a double shot of bourbon. What should I do?"

The owner, without looking up, grumbles, "Charge 'im 20 bucks."

The bartender returns to his post, pours the drink and sets the glass in front of the cat, saying, "That'll be twenty."

The cat tosses a bill on the bar and laps silently from his glass.

The bartender tries to remain casual, wiping down the bar, but finally unable to contain himself, says, "We don't get too many tomcats in here."

"Charge twenty bucks for two shots of whiskey, it ain't surprising," the cat retorts.

with humans for thousands of years, and have done so without benefit of specially prepared cat cuisine from their masters' kitchens.

Here are some general principles to consider in feeding your cat:

1) Use a premium dry cat food as the staple of your pet's diet. Dry foods have been formulated to contain ideal

rations of nutrients for animals. You can mix half a can of wet cat food in from time to time, as a treat. Just make sure you don't let the wet food spoil in the bowl.

2) Ensure your cat always has sufficient drinking water. I believe that pure spring water is superior to standard tap water. I use boiled tap water. Change the water daily.

3) Cats can become bored with the same food day after day. Therefore, it's a good idea to mix in different foods occasionally. I mix in a bit of wet food with the dry food. But once you open a can of wet food, do not keep the remainder longer than 24 hours in the refrigerator. And wet food that isn't consumed by a cat in its meal should be tossed out immediately.

4) Hydration is critical to a cat's health. If your cat never seems to drink, one way to ensure it is sufficiently hydrated is to feed it canned cat food, which contains a high percentage of water.

5) If you change your pet's diet, do so gradually over several days by mixing the new food in with the old. This will help the cat adjust without suffering unduly from digestive disorders.

6) It's a bad idea to make it a practice of feeding your cat scraps from your own meals. Besides teaching it a bad habit of begging, human food largely is detrimental to a cat's diet, and over time can cause problems with its liver and kidneys, stomach and bowels.

7) If you do give your cat a treat from your own meal, make sure the snack is fresh and served at room temperature. And if it's meat, always make sure there are no bones that could cause choking.

8) Meat products should be cut into thin strips so the animal can chew it and not swallow it whole.

9) Fish products should be given rarely, and only in boiled form.

10) Once or twice a week you can give your cat a fresh egg, either fried or boiled.

11) Dairy products contain lots of protein, but cats react differently to dairy. Some love the taste of cottage cheese or solid cheese. A spoonful of fresh cream or sour cream is a delight to some cats. In any event, as with fish, dairy products should be given sparingly.

12) Milk is not toxic to cats, but can cause adverse effects such as cramps, diarrhea, and gas. Like people, many cats are lactose intolerant. Properly fed adult cats don't need milk. If your cat begs for milk, know that the more fat content, the less lactose. A small amount of cream two or three times a week is acceptable. Pet stores and supermarkets often carry CatSip, a product composed of skim milk and an added enzyme that helps a cat digest lactose.

13) Some cats like bread. I've found that some cats especially savor black rye, which especially goes well with fish.

14) Certain vegetables, beans, and fruits (such as melons) can be given as an occasional treat to cats that like these foods. Permissible vegetables include cabbage, carrots, cucumbers, green lettuce, and summer squashes.

15) The following is a partial list of foods that are harmful to a cat and should never be fed to your pet.
    • Alcohol.
    • Candy and other sugary foods.
    • Chocolate. (Theobromine, a component of chocolate, is toxic to cats, as well as to dogs and certain other species.)

Accidental Nibbles Lead to Strange Tastes

Some cats have rather curious tastes in food. And in some cases they discover these tastes quite by accident.

I used to play a game with one of my cats, poking a stick toward her and having her bat at it and wrestle with it. One day I used a carrot instead. She sank her teeth into the orange vegetable and tasted its pulp. That was all she needed—she found she liked it. Ever since, she's eaten crunchy raw carrots.

I don't feed carrots to this cat every day. I add them occasionally to her food bowl as treats. But it always gives me a little thrill to see how eagerly she attacks these pieces of produce. And I've noted she has suffered no ill effects from these nontraditional cat snacks.

Her tastes truly are uncommon. I've tried seeing whether other cats like carrots. I might as well have tried feeding them sticks.

- Coffee and other caffeinated products.
- Salted food.
- Seasoned food. (Onions, garlic, and related root vegetables can destroy red blood cells in a cat.)
- Smoked food.
- Tomatoes, eggplant, and raw potatoes. They contain the glycoalkoloid solanine, which is poisonous to cats and can cause violent gastrointestinal symptoms.

. . .

YOU'LL KNOW YOUR CAT is on the right diet by its appearance. A healthy cat appears sinewy and well fed—neither fat nor thin.

Feel its body. If its ribs or spine bulge out, the cat's too thin. If you have trouble feeling the bones through the fur and flesh, the cat is too fat. Its skeletal frame should by covered by a thin layer of fat.

Providing your cat a proper diet greatly boosts its chances for a long healthy life, just like a person. But remember: Each cat has different tastes. If it absolutely refuses to touch certain food you give it, you must find a replacement. With effort, nourishing food can be found for the most finicky of felines.

🐾 PAW PRINTS 🐾

- A normal cat consumes between 125 and 250 grams per day.
- Adult cats eat twice a day, usually in the morning and the evening. Kittens eat more frequently.
- Cats are carnivores; their natural diet consists of about 30 percent protein.
- Cats, like people, have personal tastes. Some eat only cat food; others like various human foods.
- Quality dry cat food provides all the nutrition a cat needs.
- Ensure your cat always has clean drinking water, changed daily. Spring water or boiled tap water is best.

- Many human foods are detrimental to a cat's health. Many cats are lactose intolerant. On the list of prohibited foods for cats are sugary foods, salted foods, seasoned foods, smoked foods, chocolate, caffeine, and tomatoes.
- A healthy cat appears sinewy and well fed, neither fat nor bony.

5

Playing with Your Cat

*"The playful kitten, with its pretty little tigerish gambols,
is infinitely more amusing than half the people
one is obliged to live with in the world."*
—LADY SYDNEY MORGAN

Cats are playful creatures. They need stimulation, especially as kittens. They also need quality time with their owner—which makes you an ideal playmate. When you're not available, the right toy can keep the cat sufficiently occupied playing by itself.

A kitten suffering from idleness or solitude, due to lack of playing opportunities, will not develop into a healthy adult cat.

Kittens are naturally disposed to playing, because it's key to their development. Their initial games as newborns instill balance and coordination, and teach them their physical capabilities and limits. They play-act attacks and otherwise mimic their siblings and mother; this behavior also establishes the family hierarchy, with the strongest cat asserting dominance.

A kitten taken from the litter too soon, deprived of social games, can become timid and antisocial. It hasn't learned how to navigate its environment, and its movements are dictated by fear and uncertainty. Nor can it interact comfortably with other cats.

A healthy kitten grows increasingly energetic and playful as it grows. It may jump to and fro, or rush around without any detectable purpose. While such mischief can disturb its owner, the kitten is merely exhibiting good mental and physical health. As the kitten gains confidence in its physical abilities, it will begin scratching or biting its owner's hands. This, too, is not a cause for alarm; the kitten is merely manifesting its play fighting behavior with which it engaged its siblings in the litter.

As amusing as these games may seem, the owner shouldn't encourage them, because the kitten, after all, is growing into an adult cat, and this behavior can become dangerous. If the kitten seizes an arm or hand, leg or foot with its teeth or strikes out with a paw, it's best to gently but firmly repel the attack with a firm "no" and then redirect the cat's attention on something other than the owner's body.

This negative reenforcement will teach the kitten not to attack its owner.

A kitten needs play sessions several times a day; an adult cat needs to play about once a day. The reason goes back to its essential nature: cats are hunters. Even though its food is provided to it, as a domesticated animal, it still must satisfy its predatory urges—and it does so by play hunting. And the game is always the same: stalking, capturing, killing with a lethal bite.

The play props can be very simple, and found around the house: a thread spool, an empty matchbox, a shoelace, a ball of wadded paper, a small ball, a rubber toy, old slippers, and so on. As long as an object amuses the kitten, doesn't have sharp edges, doesn't contain a harmful substance and isn't so small the kitten could swallow and choke on it, it is appropriate. Toys also help satisfy the kitten's aggressive urges, and spare your clothing, furniture, and curtains from potential mauling and gnawing.

Just as you set aside a corner of your home for your pet's private sanctuary, designate this area or another area as one where the cat is allowed to carry off its toys. It will be a safe haven where the cat's belongings are not removed by you.

THE FOLLOWING ARE TOYS for the cat to play with by itself. The cat will chase these around, sometimes tossing them up with its paws. They are ritual games, and usually don't last long, depending on the cat's mood.

- Ping-pong balls, tennis balls or other small balls, or a cloth mouse from a pet store. You can make the toy even more desirable to the cat by spraying the object with catnip. Just remember that the smell may fade over time and the cat may lose interest in it. The scent also will erode in a toy containing loose catnip.
- A ball of yarn. Just make sure to keep on eye on your kitty, since some cats love to eat thread.
- A ball of aluminum foil (rolled up tightly enough so the cat can't unravel it and swallow bits of metal).
- A cardboard tube, such as those that come in the center of rolls of paper tissue or towels. Or a tube from a

package of wrapping paper. You can tape a cat treat inside, and the cat will play with the tube until it reaches the treat. You also can attached colored packing tape to the tube.

- A cardboard box, large enough for the cat to fit into, as well to as drag objects into. I've watched two cats play hide-and-seek with each other, using a box. Ensure the box is durable so that a cat's play, or chewing, won't destroy it.
- Sheets of newspaper. Some cats can't resist rustling inside newspaper or stacks of paper, loving the sound and the sensation. For an extra enticement hide a toy beneath some of the sheets.
- An extra-long, narrow, brown paper bag, such as used in stores selling bottles of wine, can entertain a cat burrowing inside.

GAMES YOUR CAT PLAYS with you are more spirited than its solitary games. But realize that cats—being independent—only play when they want to. Merely dangling its favorite toy in front of its nose isn't a guarantee your cat will accept your invitation. The cat must be in a good mood and completely trust you.

Pet suppliers are a great place to find interactive toys such as feathers, balls, string toys, and much more. Make sure your cat has an assortment of toys to play with and to suit its moods.

When playing with your cat, here are a few points of caution:

Most cats do not like you to be too rough with them. They

are very sensitive creatures and deeply resent being physically controlled or bullied.

If your cat is lying on its back, looking up at you, exercise caution! If you touch its belly, it may clamp its teeth on your hand and simultaneously scratch the hand with its kicking rear paws. Cats get great pleasure from this little game of theirs. In fact, they will try to entice you into playing it often by rolling over onto their backs.

Do not take advantage of your cat physically, including while playing. A cat raised by a loving, concerned owner, free of teasing or cruel mistreatment such as being kicked or tossed, usually feels secure and tranquil in human hands. In fact, a cat may not realize that people can cause pain. But as soon as this trust is shattered, it will take much time and great patience and kindness to rebuild the relationship. A cat will never forget a bad experience. In fact, its species is renowned for bearing grudges.

If you do tussle with your cat—say, by spinning it around with your hand as it lies on the ground—make sure you don't agitate it to the point it will leave scratches or tooth marks in your flesh. (If the cat does seize your hand in its teeth, relax the hand and don't resist; usually the cat will sense this and release its bite.) And don't do anything that could physically harm the animal, such as seizing it or lifting it by its legs.

While we're on the subject of touching, keep in mind that many cats don't enjoy prolonged petting. Your cat may purr contentedly for a minute or two while being stroked, then suddenly turn and bite your hand. If you pay attention to physical cues, you may detect the cat's breathing increasing in rate and the tail becoming agitated and tapping against you. That is a warning for you to cease the petting at once—or else!

. . .

THE GAMES I PLAY with my kittens are part of their first training for a possible career on stage, performing tricks in the World Famous Popovich Comedy Pet Theater.

I learned early on while developing my cat act that each cat has a natural predisposition toward certain actions. Some love to walk around my feet; others jump onto my arm; others carry toys in their mouths. And so on. I played with each kitten accordingly, and over a period of weeks and months—exercising great patience and rewarding each feat with praise and encouragement—I turned each willing kitten into a trained performer fit for the stage. (Of course, there's no guarantee after the curtain rises that a cat will respond on cue to engage in its stunt. That's why I have cats trained as backups. I discuss this in Chapter Six.)

My advice to you is to study your cat's natural habits. If it is a jumper, or a leg circler, or even a retriever, devise simple games based on that behavior. (I will address this subject in depth when I explain how to teach your cat tricks in Chapter Seventeen.)

One popular game for cats is being chased. Your cat may initiate this game, and if you're perceptive enough (and have the energy), you'll interpret its actions and join in. If your cat is staring at you, then goes and hides behind a curtain, it wants you to go find it there. Or if the cat tears like a bullet through the entire room and ends up in an opened closet, then peeks out at you, that's your prompt to pursue it. Some cats choose to play this game at a specific time each day—perhaps late in the evening when you're ready for bed!

Some cats manifest doglike behavior in that they like to play fetch. You can find out whether your cat is a retriever—and train it to retrieve—by playing a little game with it.

Take a small toy that is a favorite of the cat's. Call the cat over by its name. (If it's a kitten, it may not know its name yet, but call it anyway.) Play a little with the toy yourself—tossing it upward, rotating it now and then. Show that you're amused by the toy.

Is the cat watching all this with interest? If so, continue playing with the toy. Then take a seat nearby and toss the toy so that it falls near the cat. Let it play with the toy a little while. When it appears that the cat may tire of this game at any moment, call the cat from your seat. If it looks up, approach the toy, pick it up and sit down again. Then toss it, as before, near the cat.

Play this game for five minutes, twice a day. Eventually, a cat will begin bringing the toy back to you after you fling it. Now you can increase the game's complexity by throwing it behind objects, or hiding it in a simple place and having the cat hunt for it.

Not every cat will take to this game, or progress beyond the initial level of bringing back a toy tossed within its sight. But whatever level you reach together, playing together will be quailty time spent between master and pet.

I MUST REEMPHASIZE THAT playing is vital to a cat's physical and mental health. A cat that doesn't play either is ailing or depressed. (Or very old; older cats play less than younger ones.)

Games can be the solution to relieving a cat of depression

or stress. The right games help an animal build confidence, and also correct bad habits such as excessive aggression. (If your kitten is beginning to scratch or bite you, consider that it is doing so out of an urge for stimulating play. Distract it

Snow's Mighty Playmate

During the time when I was on the road with the Shrine Circus, still developing my pet theater act, I encountered a very strange and perplexing problem. One morning I returned to the dressing room to prepare my cats for the show, and found that one of the cages' door was open. Snow, the cage's occupant, was outside, playing around on the floor of the room. How did she get out? Had I carelessly left her cage door ajar?

That night, my wife and I took pains to insert all our cat's cage-door latches in their slots and double-check them. But the next morning, Snow's cage again was unlatched. She was out there on the floor again.

Now this was a riddle for me to solve! It was impossible for her to free herself; the walls of her cage had close wire mesh with openings too small for her to slip her paw through, were she even inclined to reach for the latch.

I wondered whether some members of the cleanup crew were coming into the dressing room and letting her out at night. So I made sure the dressing room was locked up tight at night and no one could get in without a key.

The next morning, Snow was out of her cage again. Now I grew nervous. This was really bothering me. I decided I would sleep in an adjacent dressing room with some of our other animals that night and listen for sounds of an intrusion in Snow's room. That way I could catch whatever culprit was playing this trick.

After the fair closed that day, and the groomers had made their rounds of the elephants and horses, tigers and dogs, and other animals, feeding them and cleaning their stalls, the fairgrounds settled into stillness. In the dead quiet I lay awake.

After a long time, somewhere around one or two a.m., my patience was rewarded. I heard rustling from the next-door dressing room. Very gently I opened the door from my room and peeked inside. I couldn't believe my eyes. An elephant trunk was stretched over the vinyl partition, the great beast's sensitive tip feeling around like a finger. It lit on Snow's cage and moved down to the latch, which it carefully lifted.

Snow, showing herself accustomed to this routine, walked out of her cage, hopped down and played on the ground. The elephant trunk continued rummaging around. It lifted some pellets of cat food and dropped them. Snow brushed up against her liberator's trunk. One terrible blow from this trunk could have flung the cat across the room, yet I sensed no such danger in the air.

In fact, Snow felt no fear from her mighty neighbor. She played along with this fantastic moving body part that was paying her nightly visits. Surely the elephant didn't mind Snow's caresses, bumps, and pawings at all; this little creature could not do damage to the trunk. The two of them got along famously. It fascinated me that an animal weighing about 10,000 pounds could interact so good-naturedly with a little 12-pound friend, and that this odd couple could be such fine companions as they whiled away the downtime of their circus existence.

with a ball or piece of rope, and it will switch its attention to the moving toy.)

Games can help a cat bond with its owner and other occupants of the home, including fellow pets. Games, therefore, are not only fun, but fulfill important functions.

🐾 PAW PRINTS 🐾

- Cats need to play to develop and maintain physical and mental health. Younger cats play more often than older cats.
- Cat toys can deter a cat from tearing up furniture, clothing or curtains.
- Toys can be as simple as an empty matchbox, a ball of wadded paper, an old slipper, cardboard tubes from rolls of paper towels, tissues or wrapping paper, or sheets of newspaper. Catnip can make a toy even more appealing.
- Make sure a toy has no sharp edges or small parts for the cat to choke on.
- Playing with your cat increases your bond with it. Games can relieve a cat's stress and depression.
- All cat games are related to its predator's drive to track and kill. A cat will track and pounce on a mouse-sized object, such as a rolled-up sock attached to a thin rope. A cat will rush at a feather waved back and forth. Some cats like being chased and found, like hide-and-seek.
- A cat must be in a good mood and trust you to accept an invitation to play. It cannot be forced to play.
- Avoid being too rough with your cat during playtime.

- Each cat has a natural habit that lends itself to a particular game. Some cats walk around its owner's feet; others are jumpers; others are retrievers. If your cat is predisposed to fetch, you can gradually train it to do so by tossing a favorite toy to it, and eventually at ever-greater distances from it.

Part II

Cat Training 101

6

The Language of Cats

"Way down deep, we're all motivated by the same urges.
Cats have the courage to live by them."
—JIM DAVIS

I grew up understanding the language of cats and dogs by virtue of being raised in a circus family, with parents who had trained animals in their act. I was an only child; the family pets were like my siblings. They were my earliest playmates (and given our traveling lifestyle, frequently my only playmates), and so I naturally grew attuned to their expressions—both vocalized and nonverbal—and even their moods. I developed what became a lifelong sixth sense, an ability to silently communicate with them, just by looking at their eyes.

From these furry friends I absorbed some critical social lessons. When I was a toddler, Timothy, a tomcat, would approach within a few feet but not let me touch him. He'd scrutinize me; finally, after he determined I was old enough to understand not to yank his tail, he would allow me to reach out and stroke him, and he'd interact with me. I received a more indelible lesson from our pet cat, Pucha.

Pucha was a big orange cat that was a constant playmate of mine. She kept me company in the trailer while my parents performed their pet act in the circus. And so one day, I was three at the time, I was playing with Pucha. We tired of the game. She walked off to eat.

After a few minutes, I was bored, so I walked up to Pucha and tried to get her to resume playing. She ignored me. I tried to pull her away. She made a growling sound. I tried again—and this time she turned her head and sank her teeth into my wrist.

I howled. Her teeth marks were left in my skin, which began bleeding. Tears streamed from my eyes. But it wasn't the pain that hurt the most. I felt a shocking betrayal. This cat and I had been playing happily together only a few minutes before. She was my friend; we always played. Now she'd attacked me. How could this be?

Distraught, I ran out to the circus performance area and waited for my parents to finish their act.

When they came off stage, I walked up to my mother.

"Mom, look," I said, sobbing. "Pucha bit me!"

"What did you do?" my mother asked.

"I was playing with her."

"And what did she do?"

"She just started eating," I said.

My mother nodded her head. Then she calmly explained that Pucha had the same right to a calm meal as we did, and that she was not to be disturbed while eating, and that was the reason she'd bit me. Pucha did not suddenly hate me; she just wanted to be left alone at that time.

As I grew older, I learned to treat the pets with great respect. I got better and better at communicating with them. My fluency in the language of cats grew enormously after I began incorporating them into my stage act. I began classifying their sounds and signs. But I already had a solid background in cat psychology, given my upbringing.

A grasp of the mind-set of the domestic cat is crucial to being able to speak and understand its language. That is why I began the section on cat training with a lesson on communication. If you expect a cat to respect your rules, then you need to respect your cat's needs and desires, too.

A Cat Never Forgets

To understand an individual cat, it helps greatly to consider its history. Its actions speak much louder than words ever could.

Masha, a cat with long, smoky fur, and big blue eyes that observe the world with great curiosity, was about six months old when I adopted her from a shelter. Whenever she's been on tour with the World Famous Popovich Comedy Pet Theater, she grows anxious about being left behind as we organize our pets in their cages to bring them to and from the show.

Masha, I suppose, picked up a bad case of separation anxiety in the shelter. Or maybe, as a kitten, she had been

(Continued)

left behind by her family—and was forever after on guard about such a disaster recurring.

The moment we start packing up the troupe, Masha will sit herself down near the door, or hop up on a suitcase. She'll make sure she's not forgotten.

There was one night, when we were traveling with the Shrine Circus, that we were organizing our suitcases and trunks in the dressing room after a show, and Masha was nowhere to be found. This was a great surprise. My wife, daughter and I walked around, calling, "Masha, Masha, Masha." The circus hands who loaded luggage off the train were already lugging our suitcases and trunks away to stow them in a separate truck-trailer heading to the next destination.

Suddenly, I heard a faint, "we-owr, w-owr" from somewhere in the room. I tried to track the source of the sound. Then my daughter said, "It's from here!" She pointed at one of the large traveling trunks in which we store costumes.

I hastily untied the ropes we always wound around the trunks to keep them from popping open en route. I popped the latches and raised the lid. Hunched down among an assortment of shoes was Masha. She'd been so intent on not being left behind in our rush to depart the room that she had decided to position herself inside a traveling trunk.

This is yet one more illustration of how a negative memory can shape a cat's mentality for the rest of its life. A cat simply does not forget a traumatic experience.

If your cat is acting in a very peculiar way, or has a very different reaction to a situation than most cats, chances are it is trying to tell you something. A devoted cat owner will be connected enough to the cat to try to figure out the meaning.

. . .

THE FIRST THING YOU must know is that cats form a deep bond with their humans. The cat understands that its owner worries about it and provides a suitable environment so that the cat enjoys a good life. The cat understands that its master will take care of it. And the cat craves a continual connection with its owner, and constantly experiences the need for close contact with its owner: to be played with, stroked or brushed, and gently spoken to. This is why it's important not only to provide a cat with adequate food and shelter, litter box and veterinary care, but also to spend quality time with it.

Yet the cat still wants its own space and to be its own individual. The cat is a naturally autonomous being and (unlike a dog) won't sacrifice its independence to conform to its owner's personality. A cat may be bribed into approaching you by the offer of a treat, and can be scared away by an obvious physical threat, but it won't respond to being ordered around. When a cat wants to be by itself or when it wants to leave the home to roam (if it is an indoor-outdoor cat), only strong (and strongly resented) physical force can deter its plans.

This is important background information for understanding a cat's language, which is expressed by vocal sounds as well as nonvocal behavior—body language. On the one hand, a domesticated cat is so bonded with its human owner that if, say, the owner leaves town for a couple days or more, the cat will become anxious due to its separation from human contact. Even if the cat has an optimal living arrangement—adequate food and water, shelter and warmth—its withdrawal from interaction with a human can precipitate a serious nervous disorder. (You need to find someone to look after your cat during your absence.)

On the other hand, a cat will go its own way whenever it likes. It may please itself by lying across its owner's knees "to talk" with its owner. But this will never occur by invitation. It only happens when the cat initiates this personal contact. (If you doubt this, try seizing your cat while it's involved in another activity and placing it on your lap. Watch it squirm and scramble down.)

No domestic animal is as expressive about its feelings and intentions as a cat. Its mood, its relation to its surroundings and its desires are conveyed with sounds and postures, motions and actions, and eye expressions.

A cat won't understand much more human vocabulary beyond its name, but it does grasp a general sense of what you're conveying by the tone and loudness of your voice. This is why using an affectionate, soft voice while petting your cat speaks volumes to it about your love. The message will be heard loud and clear. You can talk to your cat about anything; the timbre of your voice will translate your mood and, on some level, your thoughts.

On the cat's part, it will consistently try to establish contact with its owner to inform the owner of its intentions and desires, and even its mood. The cat communicates these feelings through body language, purring, distinct cries, and unique gestures.

If an owner can decipher a cat's sounds and signs, and if the owner can converse clearly with the cat, a very close relationship will be established. A healthy state of mutual appreciation and understanding will exist.

Since I use cats in the World Famous Popovich Comedy Pet Theater, my communication with cats is critical to earn-ing a living. For each trick I perform, I bring along one or two cats as backups—just in case. I approach a cat on its perch to begin a stunt, and take stock of its alertness. Does it respond actively to my approach? Is its tail swaying (showing its readiness), or is it flat? If the cat appears lackadaisical, I look immediately into its eyes. If its gaze is distracted or otherwise reveals lack of interest, our silent conversation runs something like this:

Me: "Well, that is your attitude?"

Cat: "Well, I'm just not feeling it today."

I immediately move on to another cat:

Me: "Well, are you game to play?"

Second cat: "Yes! Yes! Let's have a little play action with each other."

And so we proceed to perform the trick together.

A BRIEF DICTIONARY OF THE LANGUAGE OF A CAT

Ears
1. Rising vertically—*I'm feeling curiosity.*
2. Inclined back—*I'm warning you (or another target).*
3. Pressed down—*I'm preparing to attack.*

Eyes
1. Focused, looking around; and then the cat starts licking its body—*I'm acting calm before I go in for the kill.* (Can also convey genuine calmness.)
2. Squinting—*I'm feeling calm; or, I'm sleepy.*
3. Pupils large—*I'm afraid.*

A cat has a wide range of vocalizations. In general, lower pitches communicate negative feelings, such as fear, pain, and aggression; higher pitches convey positive feelings such as tenderness, comfort and complacency. Some breeds, such as Siamese, are far more talkative than others.

Purring

1. Steady purring—*I'm relaxed and content.*
2. Short bursts of purring—*Hello;* or, *I'm making a request of you. (Such as, "Feed me.")*
3. Short trill—*I feel joy or deep comfort.* (This sound is first heard in kittens as they suckle.)
4. Soft purring, followed by dissatisfied grumbling—*I've lost my patience.*

Additional vocalizations

1. Steady grumbling—*I'm dissatisfied.*
2. Restrained grumbling while feeding its kittens—*I'm warning my kittens there is apparent danger.*
3. Short cry—*I'm afraid.*
4. Howling—*I'm angry!*
5. Hissing—*I'm ready to protect my food, water or space, or to defend myself.* Or: *I've had enough of your petting me. It's gone on long enough. Stop!* (Know that many cats that enjoy being stroked will purr happily for a minute or two, but then will tire of it. Some, without any apparent warning, may turn their heads and bite your hand.)
6. Gentle meow—*Hello.* Or: *I'm making a request.*
7. Dissatisfied meow—*I'm upset.*
8. Teeth chattering/chirping sound—*I see a bird (or squirrel or other object that fires my hunting instinct).* (Animal specialists say there may be a link between the chirp-

ing and the bite a feline in the wild will use on its prey's neck.)

Physical gestures

1. Stroking a person with a paw—*I feel close to you; I feel tender toward you.*
2. Rubbing against a person—*I'm showing you love, devotion, kindness.*
3. Butting head against a person—*I'm showing you love, devotion.* Or: *I'm needing affection.*
4. Loud scratching of claws—*I want attention.*
5. Arching the back—*I'm irritated; I'm scaring off an enemy; I'm ready to defend myself.*

Tail

1. Limp—*I'm tired.*
2. Held low—*I'm disappointed, or I'm feeling aversion.*
3. Entire tail bent—*I'm dubious this interaction is going to end well.*
4. Tip slowly moves—*I'm interested (in whatever it is I happen to be looking it).*
5. Twitching—*I'm angry.*
6. Horizontal and motionless—*I'm prepared to attack.*
7. Vertical—*I'm satisfied.*

Bodily excretions

Cats communicate with each other by marking their territory with odors from their glands, claw scratches, saliva, and waste products. These smells convey messages to other cats, such as: *I have established residency here, so you might as well not proceed any farther unless you want an encounter with me.*

When your cat circles your legs and rubs against you, it's

leaving an odor from the sebaceous gland near the base of its tail.

If you see a cat leave its droppings on the ground without burying them, it means the cat is at the highest rung of the local hierarchy. The other cats will cover up their droppings, acknowledging their subordination.

Besides the cues and vocalizations mentioned above, you should know that each cat employs its own individual verbal and body language to establish a connection with its surroundings and to communicate with others, including its owner. Thus, each person can have a unique experience with a cat, and develop a very personalized dialogue.

When you become proficient at interpreting the language of cats, your cat's actions will no longer seem to be random.

WHAT TO EXPECT IF YOU OFFEND A CAT

A key to understanding dogs is that they believe they're people. A key to understanding cats is that they believe they're gods. And as the mythologies of many cultures warn us: You better take extra caution if you offend the gods.

The famous literary couplet, "Heaven has no rage like love to hatred turned/Nor hell a fury like a woman scorned," has a feline counterpart: "Hell hath no spite like a cat disrespected."

And I'm speaking of all breeds. Whether it's a frisky, talkative Siamese or a sweet, lazy Persian, it is a cat, first and foremost. If you violate its sense of honor, or fail to carry out what it perceives to be your obligations to it, it will register its displeasure in great measure. Its behavior is governed by its individual personality, but can range from annoyance to outright hostility.

- It may ignore you, as if you don't even exist.
- It may set you up for a rebuff. For example, it may lie on its side as if it were dying, and when you foolishly come to comfort it, it will turn away, its rear toward you.
- It may act out antisocially with a little display of vandalism. It may leave a puddle or droppings in the house, shake earth from a flowerpot, or shred a piece of clothing or other personal item of the offending person.
- It may scratch you or even bite you.

So intense are a cat's feelings, it can even elect to ostracize you for an extended period.

Martin, my old tomcat that I've retired from working with the World Famous Popovich Comedy Pet Theater, was outraged one day when I didn't respond to his nagging to be fed. He circled my feet as I intently remained at my computer screen. He raised the volume of his meowing—but his entreaties were to no avail. I continued ignoring him.

When I looked down at him a few minutes later, Martin was sitting at the side of my armchair. I noticed a dark puddle next to him. He looked up with an expression of childlike innocence, and then walked off.

But he wasn't about to let even that act of retribution square our differences. The rest of the day he acted as if I were invisible. He wouldn't so much as glance at me sideways. Yet he went out of his way to fawn over my wife, and even let my then small daughter play with his tail. Now, a cat's tail is its sign of authority. Try grabbing the tail, and you risk the worst rage of a feline—from hissing to scratching to biting. A cat won't even forgive a child of this frivolity. Yet Martin made a show of letting little Anastasia grab his tail.

His message to me was loud and clear: He held me in

contempt. It would take many acts of kindness on my part to make amends.

A Model Cat That Understands Counting

The individual cats in my life have frequently proved themselves to be more perceptive than I initially realized they were.

Zuzu, one of my performing cats, is very friendly, easygoing, and cooperative. She is a beautiful combination of white and brown fur. When patrons exit their seats at the V Theater after a showing of the World Famous Popovich Comedy Pet Theater and step into the lobby, they have the opportunity not only to buy DVDs with scenes from my show, but to have their photograph taken with Zuzu.

My daughter, Anastasia, will cradle Zuzu as the cat placidly poses next to the show-goer. Zuzu is very obliging and considerate, allowing adults and children both to approach her and pet her without shrinking away or giving any hint of annoyance. Max, one of the members of my stage cast, will point the camera, count, "One . . . two . . . *three!*" then snap the photo. Zuzu understands she is to face the camera.

But to my perplexity, I began noticing that in the Polaroid snapshots that resulted, Zuzu would not be looking at the camera. Her face would be turned away. Yet when I observed the photos being taken, Zuzu appeared to be staring straight at the lens.

Well, I decided to correct this problem. I held Zuzu myself, pointing her carefully toward the camera. But I noticed that even then, the photos came out with her face tilted away.

I finally solved the mystery. A bright flash is used on the camera, and this burst of light is not the most comfortable thing for anyone to endure, including Zuzu. After awhile she'd figured out the process. Whenever Max said, "three," Zuzu would instantly turn her head to the side. A split second later she'd face the camera again. This took me some time, and very close observation, to figure out.

I had to admire Zuzu's precise timing, her close listening to Max's change of inflection in his singsong countdown, and her power of deductive reasoning. Also, her diplomacy. She'd found a way to avoid the discomfort of modeling for the camera, while still managing to keep her master happy by cooperating with the photo shoot.

That, in a sense, is genius.

🐾 PAW PRINTS 🐾

- A cat understands its owner cares for it, and a cat wants close, continual communication with its owner.
- Although a cat desires closeness with its owner, it still craves its independence and won't sacrifice its individuality to please its owner.
- A cat doesn't understand many human words beyond its name, but gets a general sense of people talk by the tone and volume.
- A cat constantly conveys its moods and desires to its owner via vocal sounds, body language, or actions— including ear or tail positions, eye expressions, purrs,

meows and cries, postures, and physical actions, such as rubbing against a person.

- After you gain a good level of comprehension of the language of cats, your cat's behavior will no longer seem so random and unpredictable.
- If you offend your cat, expect that it will register its displeasure. Its intense feelings can spur a variety of vengeful acts—from ignoring you for a while, to relieving itself outside its litter box, shredding a piece of your clothing, or even attacking you.

7

Litter Box Training

*"The only mystery about the cat is
why it ever decided to become a domestic animal."*
—Sir Compton Mackenzie

Cats are naturally conscientious of their cleanliness, and even kittens want to practice good hygiene. Unlike puppies, kittens don't need to be carefully housebroken; they just need to be introduced to the litter box and their instinct will take over.

In the wild, cats find a soft spot of soil, such as sand, do their business, and then bury the droppings (unless leaving it is a sign of their dominance in the feline hierarchy). Most kittens, therefore, will happily use the litter box, as long as it is accessible and the filler is not unbearably soiled. Your task is to provide the cat with access to the box, and to regularly clean it.

While you want an out-of-the-way place for the litter box,

be sure that the location is not uncomfortable, such as a cold concrete floor in the basement. The area must be relatively quiet; loud noises or intense motion or shaking—such as from a washing machine or dryer, or traffic on a noisy street—can distract or frighten a kitten. A spot near a back door, or a quiet spot in a hallway or bathroom, often works well. Just remember that no doors should be closed that would shut off the kitten from reaching the box.

 If your kitten hasn't gotten into the habit of using its litter box, you should ease up on the rules and let it read and smoke inside.

If you have more than one floor in your home, and the kitten travels on these floors, it's best to keep a box on each floor at the start. A kitten has tiny legs, and if a box is too far away, it may decide it's not worthwhile seeking it out.

The litter box must be easy to enter and exit for the small animal. When it's grown, it can use a standard, store-bought open box. But when it's still tiny, consider using a small cardboard box, unless you have decided to use a closed box. Don't pour too much filler into the box, lest the kitten sink into it.

As with older cats, make sure the box remains clean. Check it daily. Whether a person or a cat, nothing is more unpleasant than to use a foul-smelling, soiled restroom.

. . .

THERE ARE ADDITIONAL STEPS to take with a kitten to ensure it uses the litter box every time and doesn't experience a relapse into doing its business elsewhere.

First, a bit of coaching is appropriate. You don't want the kitty to use the soil in your potted plants, or to do its business on other soft surfaces outside the box. Therefore, every time the kitten has marched up to its litter box and used it, reward it with pats and kind words of praise. A kitten responds positively to such encouragement, just like the rest of us. Just be sure to wait until it has finished its matters, so you don't distract it. And don't praise it too loudly or energetically, or it may misunderstand and flee from you. Similarly, too soft a voice won't interest it. As mentioned in Chapter Three, always speak to your cat in a calm, friendly tone. You'll know you've struck the right tone when the cat responds to your praise by approaching you, rubbing its head against you and purring.

From time to time, a kitten still will have an accident outside the litter box. Resist the impulse to swat it, poke it in the nose, or scold it. This behavior will only force it to fear you. What's more, the kitten may mistakenly associate the act of relieving itself with punishment from you if it does so in your presence; that could prove counterproductive if it is afraid even to use its litter box when you're around. In fact, it may decide to do its business in a secluded area, out of sight from you.

The proper reaction to the kitten's attempt to relieve itself outside the litter box is to calmly catch it and carry it to the nearest litter box and plant it inside. If it finishes its business there, praise it. If not? Well, there's always next time. If you do catch the kitten too late at the scene of the crime, the best method of punishment I know of is to place it in a confined area, such as in a room behind a closed door, so that it understands it is in detention of sorts. It will associate this restriction of freedom with its previous act. (This punishment must come within a few minutes, and no longer than five minutes of the misdeed, or the kitten won't understand why it is being punished.)

To clean a mess outside the litter box, use a special urine odor remover, available from pet suppliers. You'll need to get at the cleanup right away; cat urine and stains can linger for a long time, and will draw the cat back to the scent. Also, avoid using an ammonia-based cleaner, because that, too, will attract the cat. Make sure you shampoo carpet that's soiled, and even mop up the floor beneath, where liquid may have seeped through.

To remove temptations of potty spots outside the litter box, hang up all house plants as is possible, so a kitten can't reach them. The soft soil is tempting; if large plants must remain in pots on the floor, you can make the soil off limits by putting a wire mesh screen over the top, or by adding a layer of gravel, or by crisscrossing the top with adhesive tape.

Survey your living area for secluded places where a kitten would love to crawl and might decide, since the area is unused, to leave a puddle. These spots include behind a sofa, easy chair, or book case. Block access to these spots with boxes or trunks.

As with all cat training, patience and diligence are the rules. They will pay off. The kitten will come to use its litter box faithfully.

A couple of final notes are appropriate here about cats urinating or defecating outside the litter box.

An adult cat angry with its master may do its business

outside the litter box—perhaps even in a quite vengeful manner, such as leaving droppings in the living room or bedroom. If this happens to you, bring the cat to the scene of the crime, and say in a strong voice something along the lines of, "Why did you do that?!" Then confine the cat with a litter box in a small area, such as bathroom with a closed door, for a lengthy period—such as a half-day, or even overnight. This incarceration is corrective punishment that should prove effective. Some cats are especially strong-willed, and may become repeat offenders. Therefore, repeat confinements are in order until the cat learns the errors of its ways and reforms.

If a cat insists on urinating or deficating in a particular spot, clear up the mess and move your cat's feeding area to the potty spot. This will discourage your cat from soiling its own eating area, which the cat will find distasteful.

A cat that repeatedly urinates outside the litter box may be suffering from a urinary tract infection and be unable to control its actions. Such an illness is rare, but the conscientious owner must take a close look at the cat's behavior. Does it appear to feel guilty about soiling the floor? If the owner suspects the urinating is involuntary, a veterinary checkup may be in order.

WHEN CHOOSING A CAT TOILET, keep in mind that the greater the size of the litter box, the better for the owner—especially if the pet is a tomcat. A new owner can be astonished at how much waste a male cat can deposit.

Litter boxes come in two basic types: closed and open. The closed boxes are preferable if the cat is of the habit of relieving itself outside the box, or splashing urine, or tossing about the litter when digging; or if the cat is timid or modest about being seen doing its business. (Cats, after all, have unique personalities.)

There are a few reasons why a closed box may be undesirable. One is if you are prone to forget to check the state of the litter. Letting it go too long may result in an enormous cleanup, as well as discomfort for the cat. One more reason is that if more than one cat lives in the home, one cat may lie in ambush for the other while it does its business in the closed box. Yet another reason—which is a clincher—is that the cat simply refuses to use a closed box. Often it's because the cat objects to the smell that collects in the closed box. For this reason, if your cat is relatively neat, I suggest using an open box.

Regarding fillers, which type is suitable for your cat? *The one the cat uses.* That's the sole test. If you acquire a kitten, it surely has gotten accustomed to a litter box already. Ask the person from whom you're getting the animal what filler has been used. If your cat isn't using the litter the way it's supposed to, try a different kind. The cat may find the current filler uncomfortable.

Fill the box about an inch deep and clean it once a day. Adjust the frequency if the box fills quickly because you have more than one cat. If your cat doesn't consistently use the litter box, try cleaning it more often. With scoopable filler, if you consistently clean the box of droppings you might have to change the filler every two or three weeks. But if the filler has grown foul or much of it is soaked or clumped, it's time to replace it.

The box itself will have to be cleaned from time to time. Know that some cleaning products are toxic to felines. Soap and water should suffice for the box. Also, plastic liners for the boxes are advisable. And avoid placing a deodorizer or air freshener close to the litter box; many cats dislike the aromas and may avoid the box. Keeping the litter box clean should be enough to prevent foul odors from being a problem. An extra step is spreading a thin layer of baking soda on the bottom of the box.

Its also a good rule of thumb to keep as many litter boxes in the home as there are cats. That way if a box is occupied, there is another option for a needy cat. A cat may also be finicky if another cat has recently used the box, and a spare will prevent any issues.

☙ PAW PRINTS ☙

- It's not difficult to housebreak a normal kitten. Introduce them to their litter box and their instincts will take over.
- Most kittens will happily use the litter box, as long as it is accessible and the filler is not unbearably soiled.
- Deter a kitten from using the soil of potted plants by placing the plants where the kitten can't get to them. Use wire mesh, gravel, or crisscrossed adhesive tape in floor pots. Deter a kitten from using secluded spots in the home, such as behind sofas, to do their business by blocking access to those areas with trunks and other obstacles. And if the kitten has chosen a certain place as its potty spot, start feeding the cat in that spot so the cat won't want to foul it.
- Praise your kitten with warm words (though not too loud) and pats on the head for using the litter box. If

the kitten has an accident outside the box, and is caught in the act or shortly after, carry it calmly to its litter box. If it does its business there, praise it. If not, consider briefly confining it in a room behind a door as punishment. Such restriction of action is effective; pokes in the nose or swats on the body only teach it to fear you, and possibly to fear doing its business in your presence, even in its litter box.

8

Bath Time:
How to Clean Your Cat

*"A cat improves the garden wall in sunshine,
and the hearth in foul weather."*
—JUDITH MERKLE RILEY

Cats in general are not high-maintenance pets. A saying I like is, "The cat is the only self-cleaning object in the house."

If only its regular licking were really all it needed to keep itself clean!

While a cat tends to its personal hygiene by constantly washing itself with its tongue, this natural cat bathing isn't enough to keep it sufficiently free of dander, dead fur, dust, and mud. You should give it a trip to the bathtub about once a month. More frequently could remove protective oils from the fur and skin.

 A female cat has caught a sparrow. "Sir, you will excuse me, but I must eat you," it tells the hapless bird.

The sparrow, thinking fast, says, "Forgive me, madam, but are not cats renowned for their immaculate cleanliness? It is indecent to dine with dirty paws. A lady always washes before a meal."

The cat considers this, then releases the sparrow and begins thoroughly licking its forepaws with its tongue.

Freed from its captor's grip, the sparrow flies off.

Ever since, cats always wash themselves after eating.

I have higher standards than most cat owners with regard to bathing, since my wards also perform on stage, and I need them to look presentable to the public. But my greatest motive in regularly bathing and grooming my cats is to maintain their optimal health.

Cleanliness is an important component of healthiness for animals, as it is for people. What's more, a cat cohabiting with people, as opposed to running wild, must meet higher standards of hygiene so as not to transmit germs or parasites in the house. Bathing is the best defense against fleas.

Bathing a cat is one of the least pleasant aspects of ownership. Cats generally dislike getting their fur wet, which means it can be a real struggle getting the cat into the tub and completing the wash. (As mentioned before in this book, each cat is unique. Some enjoy soaking in a bath or floating in a pool; but these animals are rare. Their owners should consider themselves extremely fortunate.)

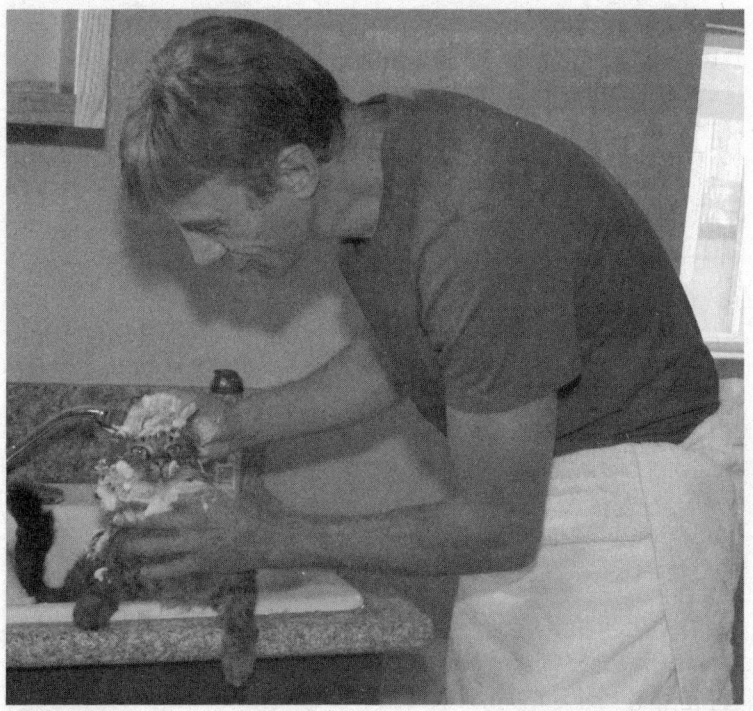

It is easier on both the cat and its owner if bathing begins in the cat's infancy. This readily accustoms the cat to the process and will limit its resistance to baths as it grows larger. Adult cats bathed for the first time not only suffer stress but also are prone to scratch or even bite, which can cause injury to its owner.

HERE ARE STEPS to take before, during and after bathing your cat, to make the experience more bearable for both of you.

Make sure the cat hasn't eaten in the past four hours. A bath can disrupt its digestion.

Before bringing a cat to the tub, trim the tips of its front claws. Even a cat used to baths won't sit still in the tub, but will squirm and attempt to flee. Better to remove the danger of sharp claws. Regular human nail clippers will suffice, or you can use cat clippers. It's best if the animal is sleepy or relaxed. You, too, should remain relaxed to not upset the cat.

Smoke.

You can wrap the cat in a towel first, cradle it in your left arm and seize the front paw with your left hand (reverse arms if you're left-handed). To make the task easier, you can have another person hold the cat while you manage the clippers. Make sure you have adequate light. Press gently on the pad to extend the claw. Snip off the clear tip, avoiding the quick—the pink area in the center, which is a blood vessel.

Calmly carry the cat to the bathroom and shut the door. Make sure the windows are shut so there is no cold draft. Throughout the bath, maintain a calm manner. As you talk to the cat, use a friendly, encouraging voice; a tone of annoyance or anger will only increase its stress and discomfort. Cats crave encouragement, so praise it for being such a trooper, and tell it how clean and beautiful it is going to look and feel.

Set out your bathing materials: cat shampoo (never people shampoo, which can dry out a cat's skin), cat conditioner (optional), a small towel and a larger bath towel, cotton balls, baby oil, a soft brush (with rounded teeth), a plastic cup, a few bright plastic toys (to distract the cat while it is bathing), and a treat such as kibble or catnip (as a reward for after the bath).

- A note about shampoo: Select a non-perfumed brand. Cats dislike smells alien to them. If they reek of lavender after a bath, you can expect the scent to be gone within 24 hours as the cat licks it away.
- A note about bath water: Some cat fanciers recommend adding a small amount of lemon juice. I disagree, for it can irritate a cat's skin.
- A special note about fleas: If your cat is infested, you will give it a special bath using anti-flea shampoo. (I prefer the Frontline brand.) Before the bath, comb out the fur using a flea comb.

You can begin by cleaning the cat's ears and eyes. A cat's ears are very sensitive, so be gentle. Wet a cotton ball (never use a swab, which can penetrate too deeply) in baby oil, pull the ear flap back and gently swap in the ear area to remove any waxy buildup. A drop of eye ointment from a veterinarian should be put in each eye, to protect against shampoo irritating the eyes.

If a cat has long fur, it should be combed out before the bath. Otherwise, loose hair will get tangled in wet fur as the cat dries.

If a cat has walked on wet asphalt, paint, resin or other adhesive, you can remove the substances by dabbing on olive oil or sunflower oil and scrubbing with an old towel. Shampoo in the bath will remove the remainder of the sticky substances.

Set a bath towel in the tub, to provide the cat traction during the bath and make it feel steadier.

Fill the tub with lukewarm water to a depth that will cover your cat's paws. Make sure no breakable objects are lying around the tub.

SET THE CAT IN the tub. When all four paws are immersed, it likely won't move around much. But if it seeks to escape, gently grasp it on the back of the neck to restrain it. Don't use so much force that the cat feels it is an act of violence. This will cause it to resist more. If it wishes to stand and place its paws on the edge of the tub, let it. If it begins straining its rear legs to prepare to leap out, you can gently clench its head under its chin and raise its face so it can't see where to jump, and it will stay put.

Before you begin the bathing, understand that you must avoid getting water or shampoo in the cat's ears. Exercise caution, and never pour water directly over the cat's head. Water in its ear canal can cause otitis.

With a plastic cup, rinse the cat until it is entirely wet. Another option is to gently using a spray nozzle, if the bath has that attachment. This will help you control the quantity of water and also avoid getting it up the cat's nose—an unpleasant feeling, and one that can frighten the animal.

Form lather with the shampoo. Try to maintain a steady rhythm without long intervals between rinsing and shampooing. This will prevent the cat from growing impatient and skittish. A cat can well endure a ten-minute bath, but anything longer will greatly upset it (and cats never forget a bad experience). Know that a soapy cat is slippery and difficult to control, so the sooner you suds it up and rinse it off, the better.

Your first soaping areas are the critical places: behind the ears, on the paws, under the tail, over the stomach, and back toward the upper part of the tail. These are the areas that will draw the cat's greatest resistance. Rinse these off. You can use tissue paper to wipe off the ears to ensure no suds remain.

Lather the remainder of the cat, avoiding the eyes and inner ears. Rinse.

If your cat has dry, brittle fur, consider using a cat conditioner. Rinse again.

Drain the water and add fresh water, and rinse again. Suds should not be allowed to dry deep in the fur, where leftover soap can irritate the skin. Ensure the fur has been thoroughly rinsed. Note: A longhaired cat may need to be bathed, then the tub drained and fresh water put in for an extra rinse, so that suds and dirt don't remain at the base of its hair.

For the final rinse, you can add a half-cup of vinegar for every five gallons of water in the tub, to help clean away remaining suds.

Pat and wipe the cat dry with the small towel, then wrap it in the larger towel. Unlike a dog, a cat can't shake itself dry. You should keep the cat wrapped in a towel for 10 or 15 minutes. Note that you should never use a blow dryer, even set on low heat. The noise scares the cat.

Once the cat is dry, brush out its fur.

Reward it with kind words and a cat treat.

ONCE ESTABLISHED, this monthly routine won't prove to be too much of a chore for you and your cat. In fact, it can become quality time together. What's more, your cat will have a lustrous coat of fur, one that will make it secretly proud.

ALTERNATE CLEANING FOR CATS UTTERLY OPPOSED TO TUBS

A cat's resistance to a tub bath depends on its personality. Some cats clearly are at the end of the spectrum of dislike (or even terror) of taking a bath. Fortunately, there is an alternative cleaning method for cats that are utterly opposed to tubs.

I have a couple of cats that absolutely hate the tub experience. They detest the bath water, and fear the rush from the faucet and spray nozzle. Even the words "bath time" send them scurrying under the couch. With these bath haters, we use a dry powder shampoo and brush out the fur. Sometimes we'll clean a dirty spot with a wet towel and shampoo. This doesn't bother these cats too much. They tolerate the cleaning. For anti-bath cats, shampoo sprays also are available.

Most cats are not extremely opposed to standard tub baths. But it's up to you, as the owner, to ensure they don't suffer a truly awful experience. It's hard enough on a cat to hear the loud unpleasant roar of water, and then to be drenched in it and be soaked by repeated rinses. (If you can think back to when you were a toddler, perhaps you can relate to the unpleasantness of having your little body scrubbed and dunked.)

Remember that cats never forget a bad experience. If you stick a cat in water that is too hot or too cold, or get shampoo in its eyes or water up its nose, it will fear and loathe baths from then on.

ADDITIONAL HYGIENIC CARE

Beyond the monthly bathing, you should tend to your cat's special cleaning and grooming as needed. As with bathing, the earlier the cat's age when the routine begins, the more quickly it will grow to tolerate it.

The following cleanings generally should be done once a week, with exceptions noted.

Brushing

Regular combing is essential to fur health. It removes dead hair, mats, and tangles, and helps new hair sprout. Long-haired cats should be brushed every other day; shorthair cats once a week. (Longhairs typically shed throughout the year; other breeds only once or twice a year. Brushing during shedding helps prevent hairballs as well as unsightly clumps on the ground.)

Brushes with wire bristles are available from pet suppliers, and vary in type to correspond to the length of the cat's hair.

Eye care

Mucus can accumulate in the corners of eyes. Swab it off with cotton balls moistened in a mixture of boiled water with a 2 percent solution of boric acid. Some people believe an infusion of chamomile should be used. I disagree. It will sting if gotten in the cat's eyes. Also, chamomile can cause excess fur to grow around the eyes.

If, when cleaning the cat's eyes, you notice tears flowing, it may be epiphora, a condition sometimes caused by a blockage of tear ducts next to the nose. A visit to the veterinarian is in order.

Ear care

Inspect the outside ear (the "pinna") for nicks or rips (often the result of fighting). If any lacerations are recent and bloody, sponge them well with a wet cloth. A serious wound can require a visit to the vet. Broken blood vessels can develop into a clot under the skin and disfigure the flap.

Inspect the pink inside of the ear by gently holding the tip between thumb and forefinger and gently rolling it outward without pulling. You're checking for signs of infection, which include redness, or dark material that looks like coffee grounds (a sign of mites). If your cat has been frequently shaking its head, flattening its ears or pawing at them, they too, are indications of possible infection—often a result of allergies or fungus, bacteria or yeast, or ear mites.

Mites cause *oititis externa*—inflammation of the outer ear canal—which can damage the inner ear and, in extreme cases, cause balance problems and deafness. The presence of mites requires a vet visit and treatment by antibiotics.

A small amount of light-brown wax is normal inside the ear. You can loosen inner wax and dirt by gently rubbing the base of the outer ear with your fingers. Squirt some feline ear cleaner (available at pet-supply stores) into the ear, and wipe it out with a cotton ball (never use a swab such as a Q-tip to poke inside). Never use water or other liquid, because it can get down into the inner ear. Clean until no more wax or dirt is inside.

Teeth cleaning

Cats fed a healthy diet often avoid dental problems such as excess plaque and gum inflammation. Dry food requires energetic chewing and promotes tooth strength.

Check inside your cat's teeth once a month for signs of infection. Bad breath alone can indicate a problem. Work under good lighting; use a small penlight if desired. Turn the cat over, cradle it and tip its head back slightly. Spread its mouth open with your thumb and forefinger. Check the back teeth for yellowing (an indication of plaque or darker tartar). Look for cracked or broken teeth. See if the gums are a full pink, not red or pale. Repeat with the front teeth. Finally, check back in the throat for redness, which may be in a cobbled pattern. That is a sign of stomatitis, a painful condition often found in older cats. Serious dental problems, including bleeding gums, should be addressed by a vet.

Clean your cat's teeth. Cat toothpaste is available from pet suppliers. You'll also need sterile gauze and a pair of scissors. Wrap the gauze around your forefinger and squeeze a small amount of toothpaste onto the tip. Take the cat in your lap. In a circular motion, gently rub its teeth, especially near the gums. Gently massage the gums. You don't need to get at the back of the teeth.

A cat that's gotten used to this cleaning can be serviced by having its teeth brushed with a small child's toothbrush.

If this is too traumatic for you or the cat, annual cleanings at the vet will suffice.

Claw care

Trimming an outdoor cat's claws is usually not necessary (except before monthly bath time, when the forepaws can be trimmed to keep yourself from being scratched).

Indoor cats may required nail clipping, which can be performed with nail clippers obtained at a pet-supply store. Make sure not to trim too low or you'll hit the quick (the blood vessel), which is painful for the cat. A good time for nail clipping is when the cat is relaxed or sleepy, and thus more likely to let you handle its paws.

The vet visit

A regular checkup is in order once a year. See the vet whenever the cat gets sick or injured and does not quickly recover.

Cat Bathing Steps—from an Interested Party

Seven easy steps to washing your cat:

1) Clean out a toilet bowl.
2) Add shampoo to the water.
3) Retrieve your cat and place it in the bowl.
4) Immediately shut the toilet lid and sit on it to prevent the cat's escape.
5) The cat will thrash around, agitating the soapsuds.
6) Flush the toilet three or four times, to ensure a thorough cleanse and rinse.
7) Open the toilet lid and bolt out of the bathroom, shutting the door behind you as rapidly as possible.

Any questions, see me.

—The Dog

FIGHTING FLEAS

No matter how clean you keep your cat, and even if it is an indoor cat, it is still susceptible to fleas. Fleas can leave a cat and bite humans and other animals, transmitting infections and other parasites, such as tapeworms.

Usually, a few fleas on a pet cause it little harm unless the pet is allergic to substances in the flea saliva. But a small animal hosting a large infestation of fleas can end up dehydrated and anemic from this condition, known as flea allergy dermatitis. Some kittens can die from a large number of fleabites.

If you notice your cat biting and scratching its fur more than usual, as if something is irritating it, you need to check its skin carefully to see if dark-brown crawling insects are present. Check the cat's sleeping area as well, since fleas fall off when a cat scratches. Small black flakes at the base of the cat's fur also indicates the presence of fleas.

The regular bath time for your cat is a chance to eradicate fleas. Flea shampoo is composed of chemicals that kill fleas. But using this shampoo requires caution to avoid irritating the cat's skin. Another bath-time technique that can be performed after the flea shampoo is brushing out the fur with a flea comb. Prepare a bowl of water with a bit of flea shampoo dissolved in it. Soak the comb in the water after each stroke to drown the fleas. A blob of petroleum jelly on the comb can help catch fleas.

Flea powders and sprays are available, but should be used under the advice of your veterinarian. Powders, for example, should be employed sparingly to avoid drying out the cat's skin and fur. Oral medicines—effective when used in conjunction with other flea-prevention treatments—can be mixed in with a cat's food to keep fleas that are feeding on the blood from having their eggs mature.

A flea collar is the most popular form of flea control. Flea collars, worn in addition to a regular ID collar, contain poison that kills adult fleas in and around the cat's head and neck. But fleas living elsewhere on the body are not affected. Topical ointments and creams are more effective. They can be obtained at the vet and usually are meant to be applied once a month.

In addition to treating your cat, the most effective way to keep your cat relatively free of fleas is to scrupulously clean your home and yard to eradicate flea breeding grounds. Fleas can hide under carpets and beds, behind curtains, and in other protected areas. Most congregate near your pet's sleeping area. Regular vacuuming of carpets, upholstery and your pet's bedding is a must. To prevent fleas from hatching from cocoons in the vacuum bag, place clipped ends of an all-natural flea collar into the vacuum bag.

You can mix white vinegar and water in equal parts in a spray bottle and mist pets, carpets and flea-infected areas. Borax applied to carpets, furniture, cat bedding and the surrounding floor is another well-known home remedy.

Another easy home remedy for killing fleas is mixing a few drops of liquid dish detergent in a bowl of water and placing it in the center of a flea-infested room. Position a bright light so that it shines onto the water as the only light source in the room. Fleas will be attracted to the light and will jump into the water. The detergent will keep them from bouncing out. They will drown.

Fleas propagate in moist environments. Keeping your yard dry and clean can eradicate flea breeding grounds. Keep the grass mowed, the shrubs trimmed, and clippings and leaves raked and removed. Don't mow your lawn shorter than two inches, lest you harm the yard's natural populations of spiders and ants—mortal enemies of the flea. Birds also feast on fleas, so installing birdhouses and birdfeeders and scattering birdseed about your grounds will attract these flea predators.

Fleas thrive in warm conditions, so in summer you should take care to wash your pet's bedding in hot, sudsy water once a week, and put the bedding in a hot dryer.

Also know that stray cats carry fleas. Welcoming a stray cat, such as leaving food out, is an invitation to making fleas at home, as well.

If your home has suffered a large infestation of fleas, you can benefit from flea bombing the house. Make sure you have enough bombs to cover the entire home, that you follow the product's directions, and most importantly, remember to remove pets from the house while it's being bombed.

❧ PAW PRINTS ❧

- Cleanliness is necessary to healthiness in a cat, as in a person. Regular bathing is the best defense against fleas.
- Baths should be on a monthly basis. The younger a cat starts with baths, the sooner it becomes accustomed to the unpleasant experience.
- A cat should not have eaten in the previous four hours before a bath.
- Trim the tips of the claws on the forepaws before the bath.

- Remain calm and relaxed, and speak kindly to the cat during the bath experience, to soothe it.
- Use only cat shampoos.
- Fill the tub with lukewarm water deep enough to cover the paws.
- Use a plastic cup or shower spray nozzle and avoid getting water in the cat's eyes, ears, or nose.
- Lather and rinse several times. Drain the water for a fresh supply to ensure there are no suds left deep in the fur.
- Pat and wipe the cat dry with the small towel, then wrap it in the larger towel. Avoid a hair dryer.
- Brush out the cat's fur.
- Reward it with kind words and a cat treat.

9

Getting Your Cat to Let You Sleep

"Only cat lovers know the luxury of fur-coated,
musical hot water bottles that never go cold."
—SUSANNE MILLEN

Kittens have a habit of crawling up on your pillow at night and curling up above your head. Other favorite slumbering spots for kittens and cats are on their master's chest or in the space between the master's sprawled legs. Pet cats crave closeness and warmth with the essential provider of their needs. What's more, a kitten newly brought into the house—taken from its mother and siblings, or perhaps adopted from a shelter after significant upheaval in its young life—is still afraid of its new surroundings and in need of comfort and security. Its yearning to sleep with you shows its trust in you.

The problem for the owner is that this sleeping arrangement

also allows the kitten a measure of control. A cat that has woken and finds its master still asleep views this as an unacceptable situation. After all, the cat has its needs to be tended to—including filling its food bowl. A cat that wants its person to stop sleeping has ways of making this happen. The cat may jump on its master's chest, walk the length of the master's body, or brush its tail over the master's face, tickling the nose into a wakening sneeze.

The most important rule for the cat owner is the same rule that applies in all cases when you must train a cat from the start to adopt acceptable behavior: If you let a cat do whatever it likes, then the cat will continue dictating to you in the future. Therefore, right at the beginning of your life together, you must set and enforce unshakable policies. In the inevitable struggle for who is going to be boss in the family, you must step up. The critical phase is the first two weeks of your relationship. Any lack of earnestness on your part, any vacillation, will only send conflicting messages to the cat. In a battle of wills with this extremely willful creature, you will find it increasingly difficult to train it in acceptable behavior if you don't assert your authority from the get go.

Kittens are quick learners. If a kitten clambers up on your chest as you lie in bed and nuzzles you awake, and you begin playing with it, and then get out of bed and feed it, the kitten will remember and repeat this act as a means of getting what it wants. You may well return to bed for more shut-eye, but the damage has been done. The next morning, you can expect another rude interruption of your dreams.

You have two sound options to nip this problem in its bud.

Situate the new cat's sleeping area far from your bedroom

I recommend a cage with the door left open and a pillow inside. It's a private place for the cat to retreat to. If the cat has come from a shelter, include some torn newspaper that was in its cage in the shelter, so that the cat will have a familiar scent and recognize its cage as its own private domain.

With its own sleeping area set up at a safe distance from your bedroom, the cat may not even figure out where you're sleeping. Keep your bedroom door closed, just in case. Should the cat ever make its way into your room, do not permit it to get on the bed, at any hour of the day.

Be prepared for a new kitten to cry for the first two or three nights. That is normal. It seeks its mother. It will get over this. When the young cat realizes the crying is futile, it will settle into its new situation. But if you succumb to your own parental inclinations to go and comfort the cat, you've set yourself up for its continual crying and whining.

Should a cat succeed in invading your bedroom and climbing onto your bed while you're trying to sleep, your course of action is to return it immediately to its own sleeping area. Ignore its cries of protest. Should it return outside your door and set about scratching, tune it out. It eventually will stop. (And woe unto you who gives in. The scratching will become ingrained in the cat as a means to get you to grant it entrance. Instead of you disciplining your cat, it will be disciplining you. Cats not only are trainable—they are determined trainers!)

Ignore or shoo away your restless pet

If your home is a small area, and there is no separate place that's convenient for setting up a cat's bed, you can allow it to sleep in your room, and perhaps even on your bed. Or maybe you just enjoy the closeness with this animal, and that's enough to make you decide to let your bed become your cat's, too. But in either of these situations you still must be strict about not rewarding the cat for undesirable behavior—such as waking you up. If you open your eyes to find your kitty staring down at you, do not begin stroking it, much less rouse yourself and set about feeding it. Best to ignore it, or shoo it

Martina Gets the Boot

Martina is a kitten we adopted as a house pet for our daughter, Anastasia. Ana let Martina sleep on her bed. The kitten nestling against Ana's shoulder didn't bother our daughter, for active teenage girls like her are sound sleepers. But then Martina found her way up onto my wife's and my bed. She crawled above my head and settled in. She evidently assumed this was allowable behavior. She swept her tail back and forth, dug her claws into the sheets, and thrashed around. I was less than amused after I woke up and discovered the source of the disturbance.

It would have been impossible to break this cat's sleeping custom, since it had been reinforced by Ana's permissiveness since Martina's kittenhood, and since Ana continued to let Martina onto her bed.

Therefore, the only sound solution was my wife and I shutting our bedroom door to keep Martina out. Thus, we regained our sound sleeping arrangement.

away. It will learn that disturbing you in bed will not bring about any favorable results.

You also should think the matter through carefully beforehand. If you permit the cat to sleep with you, it should be a permanent policy. Banishing it from your bed and forcing it into a new arrangement several months down the line will be confusing and traumatic for it.

🐾 PAW PRINTS 🐾

- A kitten new to your home and still unsure of its surroundings may crawl onto your bed, perhaps by your head, to sleep. This shows its trust in you.
- Giving a cat its own sleeping area far from your own will keep it from disturbing your sleep. A new kitten may cry for two or three nights, but if you ignore it, it will quit the crying after getting used to its new home.
- A cat sleeping in your bed with you will try to control you by waking you when it wants to play or eat. The easiest solution to not having sleep disturbed is to give your cat its own sleeping area. Close your bedroom door. Ignore any scratching.
- If you do let a cat sleep in your bed, do not reward it for waking you. Do not play with it or feed it. It eventually will quit trying to rouse you.
- As with all training of your cat, the earlier you start, the easier it will be. Bad habits are difficult to break.

10

Teaching Your Cat to Not Damage Furniture

"In a cat's eyes, all things belong to a cat."
—ENGLISH PROVERB

This question arises for almost every cat owner at some point: *Why does my cat tear up my upholstery?*

The answer they frequently come up with is: *Because it's sharpening its claws.*

This isn't entirely correct. A cat isn't honing its claws for a reason similar to that for which we sharpen knives. The scratching of furniture (or curtains, carpet, wallpaper, or other pliable surfaces) serves four purposes.

1) The cat is scraping off the old worn shells of its claws to release young, new claws. The process is akin to shedding dead layers of skin. This should be comforting

information to owners alarmed at finding pieces of claw stuck in the durable cloth of a sofa or chair, and believing their cat has a wounded paw.

2) The cat is training and strengthening its paws' ability to push out and retract the claws—vital for gripping objects, climbing trees, and fighting.

3) The cat is stretching itself out (which feels good and is necessary to its health) by pulling and working the muscles of the front quarters.

4) The cat is marking its territory. The scratches leave the cat's signature smell. The front paws contain glands that secret an aromatic substance. The motion of clawing allows the glands to rub against the surface being clawed, and the scent permeates the grooves. (If scratches disfigure your favorite armchair, regard it as a sign of your cat's devotion: It has added its personal smells to yours.)

AS WITH ALL BEHAVIORAL training of your cat, the sooner you get started, the better for each of you. Cats start claw sharpening, using their teeth as well as surfaces, in their first month of life. Proper training against scratching the furniture or walls should begin when it is a kitten, and be reinforced with words of praise when the kitten uses the scratching post instead of the living-room couch.

Scratching posts can be bought from a pet supplier, or fashioned yourself. Here are the main considerations when procuring and setting up a scratching post:

• Some cats sharpen claws by stretching high and scraping the nails down along a surface, while others are in the habit of dragging nails across a carpet. Your cat's preference determines if you choose a vertical or horizontal scratching post. (You may opt to provide both for your cat.)

- The post's surface must be high enough or long enough to suit the cat. (Posts from stores typically range from two to three feet high, and are set on a wide base.) The easiest way to determine the proper dimensions is measuring the surface where the cat has been scratching. Is it your sofa? Take a tape measure to it.

- Scratching posts come in different surfaces. Select the one most similar to the surface on which your cat has been scratching. Store models usually are covered with tough upholstery fabric, sisal (hemp) rope, or jute (such as commonly used as carpet backing).

- Some commercial posts are quite elaborate, with platforms set on different levels, and having recessed hiding areas. Tall models are called "cat trees." There are many variations of posts, including an inclined scratching block treated with catnip and with a mouse toy suspended inside.

- You can build your own scratching post. A very simple design involves a piece of carpet flipped backward and suspended by a loop from a doorknob. Instead of carpet, you can substitute a panel of corrugated cardboard. If your cat likes scratching on wood (such as your doors), consider bringing in a tree log with rough bark. Another option: a wooden sawhorse.

- Cats don't like moving surfaces. Make sure your post is sturdy enough that it won't wobble when scratched.

- Buying several varieties of scratching posts for your cat allows your pet to enjoy different surfaces as it likes.

Place the post in a spot accessible to the cat, and where it typically hangs out, such as next to the piece of furniture it has been digging into. (If this isn't the most pleasing location for you, just wait until the cat has permanently switched to the post as its scratching surface, then gradually move the post toward its final destination, shifting it a few feet each day.) An excellent alternative location is next to where the cat sleeps. Many cats engage in their nail sharpening soon after waking—scratching on whatever surface is nearby. Orient your cat to the purpose of the post by running your own fingernails over it, as the cat watches.

My cats lounging on a cat tree.

If you notice the cat continuing to use your furniture instead, you can up the ante by hanging an old sweater or a cloth of some kind on the post. You also can spray catnip on the post. When your cat uses the post, remember to reward it with warm words of praise. This step is extremely important in reinforcing good behavior.

Unfortunately, if the problem isn't addressed early enough or decisively enough, the scratching up of your furniture may continue. If the cat already has selected a favored place for whetting its nails, changing its behavior can prove difficult. Here are three suggestions:

1) Stick double-sided adhesive tape where the cat loves to scratch. You can try the tape used for carpet installation, or special sticky strips available from pet suppliers. Your cat will not be pleased with the tape sticking to its paws, and will refrain from scratching there.

2) Herbal spray deterrents also can be bought from pet suppliers, and applied to places you want to keep your cat from scratching, such as the upholstery.

3) Using a water pistol or other sprayer, hit the cat with a jet of water whenever it is sharpening its claws on a prohibited surface. Another form of negative reinforcement: Raise your voice. (The only drawbacks to these methods is that the cat may mistakenly believe you oppose all claw sharpening, and therefore resist even using its scratching post in your presence.)

SOME CAT OWNERS EMPLOY severe measures to eliminate furniture scratching: They have their cat's nails surgically removed. The debate over declawing is one of the more impassioned ones among cat owners. I am firmly against declawing. There are valid reasons for altering a pet's nature when it comes to its ability to reproduce. Spaying and neutering are humane practices, given the vast number of unwanted offspring that are put to sleep every year. But removing a cat's claws is as cruel as amputating a person's fingertips, severing them at the third knuckle.

True, you won't suffer your cat's scratch marks on your couches or curtains anymore. But your cat will never be the same. It will endure a lengthy healing process; because it has no choice but to limp around on its paws, it will experience pain until the healing is complete. (This could take up to two weeks, or longer in some cases.) Even kneeling on its paws will be unpleasant. You might not even realize how much hurt is involved, for cats bear their pain stoically.

After being declawed, a cat very well could undergo a personality change. Its primary form of protection has been taken from it, and it may become irritable. It may begin to bite. If the surgery was not competently carried out, the cat can experience a host of additional problems, including chronic pain, a gimpy gait, and various infections.

Sometimes only the front paws are declawed, leaving the rear ones intact. This allows a cat some means of defense and climbing ability; but a cat with front paws declawed still undergoes a period of adjustment. When it tries climbing and running along elevated areas, it frequently will lose its balance or fall.

Declawing is uncommon and even illegal in many countries outside of North America. The European Convention for the Protection of Pet Animals bans declawing except where the animal's medical condition requires it. A cat may be suffering from tumors, gangrene, or severe infections in a distal phalanx. A veterinarian will customarily remove only the bone holding the affected claw.

One other situation seems reasonable for declawing: If the cat's owner has a weakened immune system and is at risk of a lethal infection if scratched by a cat. These owners may be suffering from AIDS or diabetes, or undergoing chemotherapy, or may have received a transplanted organ. The motive for declawing this person's cat is to avoid having to sever the master-pet bond by finding the animal a new home.

. . .

A METHOD NOT AS DRASTIC as declawing, yet still inhumane in my mind, is tendonectomy.

This involves surgery that cuts the digital flexor tendon of each claw, thus preventing the cat from moving its distal phalanges and baring its nails. This procedure will result in less pain for the cat after operation, but it still will suffer lameness, bleeding, and possible infection during the recovery period. The cat also will experience the physical (and emotional) loss of an ability to climb, cling, and defend itself. The American Veterinary Medical Association does not recommend this surgery as an alternative to declawing.

Since the cat won't be able to draw out its claws for grooming or for wearing them down naturally, the owner must regularly clip the cat's nails to prevent claws from growing into the paw pads, which will cause pain and infections.

TWO REASONABLE ALTERNATIVES to surgery are available to owners who haven't been able to train their cats to not scratch up the home:

1) Vinyl nail caps. These are attached over claws using nontoxic glue. These caps must be replaced every four to six weeks or so, when the cat sheds its claw sheaths. Two brands are Soft Paws and Soft Claws.
2) Regular trimming of your cat's nails, to blunt the sharp tips.
   This last method is by far the preferred one in my book.

🐾 PAW PRINTS 🐾

- Cats begin sharpening their claws in their first month of life, and for multiple purposes: scraping off old shells, strengthening clawing ability, stretching front quarters, leaving their scent.
- The earlier you begin training your kitten not to scratch furniture, carpets, and other forbidden areas, the better. The best remedy is providing a scratching post.
- Choose a scratching post with a surface similar to the surface the cat has been scratching. You can buy a post from a pet supplier or build your own.
- Make the scratching post accessible to your cat. Demonstrate scratching on it the first time the pet sees the post. Position the post near the area where the cat has been scratching. Over a course of several days you can gradually reposition the post farther away, until it's in the desired area. One good area is next to where the cat sleeps.
- If your cat persists in scratching elsewhere after a post has been provided, you can shoot the cat with a water pistol or other sprayer when it begins the offensive action. You can raise your voice, as well. Other deterrents include employing double-sided adhesive tape, or herbal sprays, on the forbidden scratch areas.
- Declawing or tendonectomy are drastic and, in many people's opinion, inhumane procedures.

11

Stopping Your Cat from Biting and Scratching

*"Some Cats is blind, and stone-deaf some,
but ain't no Cat was ever dumb."*
—ANTHONY HENDERSON EUWER

Scratching and biting are natural behaviors of cats in the wild. They are, after all, born predators, and successful ones at that.

A cat's teeth and claws are designed for hunting and fighting, and used as well in defending itself or extricating itself from a dangerous or uncomfortable situation. A cat's instincts never leave just because it's domesticated. Therefore, it is impossible to train your cat to never scratch or bite, any more than you can train a fish not to swim. Your sole concern as a cat owner should be to moderate overly aggressive behavior in your pet. A good place to start is with your own behavior.

Are you giving your cat justifiable cause to use its natural weapons against you? For example, are you holding a small kitten in your hands and not releasing it as it struggles and squirms to get free? Are you holding a cat in your arms too long, stroking it beyond its threshold for appreciating such stimulation? Certain actions trigger a cat's biting and clawing response. Grabbing or pulling its tail, for example. Stroking it in a spot that's uncomfortable for the cat, like its paws or belly. Or simply playing too rough with it.

If a cat is old or sick and feeling vulnerable, it may not take much more than you coming too close to it to prompt it to lash out. Sometimes an unexpected attack—such as the cat pouncing on your leg as you pass, and clawing and biting—is your cat's way of communicating to you that it is ailing. (As I've said before, cats handle pain stoically; you must be attuned to signs of illness, such as a diminished appetite, or the cat pulling fur from its chest.) In this case, you should arrange a visit to the vet.

Occasionally you may simply encounter a cat that is in a foul or bitter mood. Maybe it has been neglected by its owner, lacking proper affection and stimulation. Maybe it has suffered abuse at the hands of people, and its fear-fueled hostility has been triggered by a sight, scent, or sound it associates with the abuse. Maybe it has wandered into a stranger's home or yard, has panicked, and is trying to escape when you innocently come upon it and try to approach it— unwittingly blocking its exit. (Cats, being of relatively small size in the food chain, fight fiercely to survive.) Maybe it is fearful of humans, in general, and perceives you as an enemy. Maybe it is a tomcat in heat, and deprived of females.

If you do suffer bites or claw marks, know that if the cat is healthy and has received its regular inoculations, you won't require special medical treatment. But you should use an antibiotic spray or ointment on your broken skin to avoid possible inflammation. Cat claws carry lots of bacteria, which is why even shallow scratches can get red and painful.

WHILE A CAT WILL exercise its right to fight tooth and nail in extreme situations, you can teach it in kittenhood to not habitually use these tools against you. You can train it to channel its aggressive tendencies in harmless ways.

The best thing you can do is to make sure your cat has ample playing time and enough toys. Therefore, it will have a heathy channel for its hunting instructs and won't be tempted to attack just any moving target.

If no one in my family has had a chance to play with one of our young pet cats during the day, when we return at night we play with it until it is exhausted enough that it lacks not only the will but the strength to muster an assault on an innocent hand or foot.

Many cat rescue organizations require people to adopt kittens in pairs, since kittens need near constant stimulation and play. If an owner has adopted a single kitten and finds him or heserlf being pounced on, scratched, or bitten, it's most likely because the kitten needs a fellow kitten to tussle with. If this is the case, you can increase your playtime with the restless kitten, or you might consider adopting a playmate to keep it engaged when you're not available.

It's common for kittens to bite and scratch, since this is how they learn to use the tools that allow them to stay alive in the wild. Usually, as kittens grow into adolescents and full-grown cats, their biting and scratching diminishes substantially. The best way an owner can respond to a kitten that likes to bite and scratch is not to encourage these behaviors. Thought it may seem cute when a cuddly little kitten attacks your hand, make sure that you and those in your household don't encourage it. Otherwise you'll end up with an adult cat that you've trained to bite and scratch, which isn't so cute.

METHODS OF COMBATTING BITING AND SCRATCHING

When playing with your kitten or cat, do not allow it to scratch or bite your naked hand or leg. Cats are creatures of habit, so it's essential that you consistently stop this nasty habit before it starts.

If the cat grows too spirited during play and uses its claws against you, simply end the game and tell the cat, in a tone it will understand (but which will not frighten it into flight), "No claws." Walk away and ignore the cat for five to ten minutes, showing it that playtime stops when the cat becomes too aggressive.

If your cat attacks you too forcefully during play, you can use negative reinforcement such as a spritz from a water pistol or other sprayer (if one is next to you; the cat won't associate this action with its own action unless punishment follows the transgression immediately), or a loud slap or rap of your hand against the table or ground other hard surface—forcing the cat, out of surprise and fright, to retreat. But it's better to use positive reinforcement, like trying to redirect the animal's energy on a toy.

Tomcats in heat will become more aggressive toward other cats, and even dogs, as well as humans. But a neutered tom doesn't suffer this manifestation of sexual energy. (And unless you're a breeder, fixing your cat is the duty of every responsible cat owner, as noted earlier.)

If you are tired of nasty scratch marks from playing with your cat, you can take another step in addition to moderating its behavior: You can trim its nails (as discussed in Chapter Eight), or cover its claws with soft tips (see Chapter Ten).

AVOID THESE HUMAN BEHAVIORS THAT TRIGGER BITING AND SCRATCHING

Don't grasp and hold the cat against its will. A cat, like a person, isn't always in the mood for cuddling or playing. Respect its right to personal space and peace.

As mentioned in Chapter Six, if you stroke your cat for too lengthy a period, such as for more than a minute, it may grow irritated and angry. It may suddenly, unexpectedly, turn and sink its teeth into your hand. If, while you pet it, the cat's tail starts moving and tapping you, that's a signal to cease your doting.

As mentioned in Chapter Five: Your cat may be lying on its back, seemingly inviting you to stroke its belly. Do so, and the cat likely will seize your hand by its front paws, bite your wrist and kick and dig its rear claws into your arm. As cute and inviting as your cat's belly may appear, you may have to resist the temptation to pet it if your cat doesn't like this form of attention.

AS A FINAL NOTE, here is a tip for extricating yourself from having your arm or leg mauled by your otherwise loving pet:

Remain absolutely passive. Just freeze, not making a sound. This is a sign of subordination to your cat. Most of them, having subdued the moving limb, will release the grip of their mouth and forepaws, and stop beating a tattoo with their sharp rear paws.

Resisting the attack, on the other hand, sends a message to the cat to increase the ferocity of its clenching and pummeling. Submission on your part will spare your skin from further damage.

As with so many interactions of the owner-cat relationship, communication is key. Knowing your cat's language so you can foresee an attack and stop it will make your relationship run much smoother.

🐾 PAW PRINTS 🐾

- Cats, being natural predators, instinctively bite and scratch, and can't be trained to give up either action completely.
- Scratching and biting frequently are a cat's response to fear. An owner can avoid being scratched or bitten by not triggering fear or aggravation in a cat.
- A cat that is sick may unexpectedly pounce on its owner's leg or otherwise use its teeth or claws—its way of communicating its illness to its owner.
- Slapping or rapping loudly on a solid surface can startle a cat and force it backward if it is attacking you.
- Remaining absolutely still and quiet if a cat has seized a part of you with its teeth or paws will signal your subordination. Most cats release their grip at this point.

12

Breaking More Bad Habits

*"Cats were put into the world to disprove the dogma
that all things were created to serve man."*
—PAUL GRAY

Your pet is a source of personal happiness and pride for
you. But there are trying moments from time to time. A
non–cat owner may scoff at the statement, "Cats are only human," but we cat owners know differently, don't we?

Cats can behave badly—whether it's the innocent clawing
of a kitten that shreds wallpaper, or the manipulative yowling
of a well-fed adult cat insistent it be served extra wet food.

While the best way to stop bad habits are to nip them in
the bud before they start, here are some methods of correcting bad behavior as it's happening:

Immediate, clear punishment

When training your cat to adopt behavior you desire, keep in
mind what was said in Chapter Seven in regard to correcting

litter-box misdeeds: Punishment must come immediately after the transgression, and at the scene of the crime, or the cat will not understand why it is being punished, and just think you are being mean. Cats, like most animals, make cause-effect connections, instead of thinking critically. So if you come home from work and find a flowerpot toppled over and broken, scolding your kitten will serve no beneficial purpose.

Another consideration to bear in mind is that you must be specific about the behavior you are trying to correct. If a cat knocks over glasses or dishes on the kitchen table, the act you are targeting is the jumping on the table, period. If the cat approaches the table in your presence and crouches, making ready to leap and mount, loud clapping and shooing away, scolding words, or a spritz with a water pistol will deter the act because the cat will link your unwanted reaction with its act of jumping onto the table.

Consistency also is essential. If you let your cat get away with jumping on the table some times but not others, or you give into its begging for food once in awhile, you're sending the cat mixed messages. This is not only unfair to the cat, but it will reinforce bad behavior.

The "mousetrap"

You can't monitor your cat 24/7. Nor, given its independent nature, should you try. But you can install deterrents to its commission of unwanted acts. Examples include covering the soil of potted plants with wire mesh or gravel (as discussed in Chapter Seven) or putting double-sided adhesive tape on couches where the cat likes to scratch (as mentioned in Chapter Ten).

Clatter deterrent

If your cat likes to jump up on the kitchen counter, try placing some baking sheets on the counter so they hang off the lip. When the cat attempts to jump on the counter, the baking sheet will topple off, making a loud clatter and scaring the cat. It's important to remember that the best way to prevent a cat from doing something is to make the act undesirable.

Remove temptation

Sometimes it dawns on the pet owner that it is the pet that trains the owner to change behavior. You can do your part to remove targets of opportunity for your cat. An obvious one: Don't leave food out on the table after a meal. Clean up in good course.

Eliminate stabs for attention

Pets, like people, can feel lonely and ignored—and may commit a purposely annoying act in order to be noticed. A dog barking for no apparent reason is a perfect example from the canine world. A cat? Brushing its tail against your face as you read. Or scratching at its door to be let out, then immediately scratching to be let in. A solution: Play more with your cat. Carve out some quality time with it. Its disruptive behavior should cease.

Some cat owners grow perplexed, and then perturbed, when the pet cries to be let out of the house, and, after a very short time, scratches or cries to be let back in—then repeats this pattern again and again, perhaps every minute. Here is a battle of wills. The cat most likely is trying to control you, having discovered a way to get its master to serve its beck and call. The solution? Ignore the cat, despite its insistent meows. Don't continue letting it out. Eventually, it will desist.

Cat Calls

Cats can prove very resourceful in managing situations. A cat that gets a notion in its mind cannot easily be outwitted by a human.

In the days before cell phones, I would sometimes be out performing on the road, while my wife stayed behind with our young daughter. I'd call home as often as I could.

On one such call I heard the receiver pick up at the other end of the line. I could hear that the call went through. But my wife's voice didn't come on the line.

"Hello, hello," I said.

No reply. Just the ambient sound from the room on the other end.

I finally hung up in frustration.

I called back later, and my wife picked up the phone. "Why didn't you answer me when I called earlier?" I asked.

"I must have been out of the home when you called. I didn't get the call," she said.

That puzzled me. But perhaps I'd dialed the wrong number, or the line had gotten crossed.

But the same thing happened a few days later. I called. The phone rang. The receiver picked up. But again, not a peep from whoever answered the phone.

"Hello!" I said loudly. "Izolda? Anastasia?"

No reply.

Now I was upset. Was there some stranger in my home, answering the phone and deliberately not speaking to me?

As before, I called back later. Same situation: My wife said she never got the previous call. This time she'd been home, but she hadn't heard the phone ring, she said.

The mystery was eventually solved. My wife kept an eye on the phone. It turned out that when it rang, our resourceful cat Snow would jump up next to the old-style telephone, watch it ring, then knock the receiver off its cradle.

Why? Well, this was no random action by the cat. I came up with two theories:

1) The dring-dring of the phone was grating on Snow's ears, so she figured out how to stop the obnoxious sound.

2) And this is a more interesting theory: When I'd call from the road, after talking with Izolda I'd often say, "OK, let me talk with my cat." Izolda would hold Snow up to the receiver and I'd say a few words to her, too. She recognized my voice coming through the receiver. She connected the phone ring with my voice being ready to speak through this object.

Well, relocating the phone to a place outside of Snow's reach proved to solve this little, and rather adorable, problem. As bad habits go, it was nothing we cared to address with the culprit herself.

Her cleverness in handling the phone was quite admirable!

HERE ARE SOLUTIONS TO two more bad habits:

Spraying

Cats, being naturally territorial, mark their territories in a variety of ways that let other cats know a cat is living there. They leave scents (undetectable by humans) from sebaceous glands on their face, paws or tail being rubbed over objects. That's why it's common to see a cat lean its cheek against a vertical object in its home territory—such as a leg of a table or side of a sofa, or a fence in the yard. Cats also leave scents and markings from claw scratchings, and tomcats spray droplets of urine.

Scents fade, so the cat must continue patroling its domain and leaving fresh identifying markers. Urine scents also are meant to attract partners during mating season. The smells in cat urine may contain a wealth of information for cats—but are very repelling to humans.

The best way to prevent your cat from becoming a sprayer is to have your pet fixed before it reaches puberty. If this is done after puberty, its spraying nevertheless should decrease.

If your tomcat is fixed yet is still having his wet way inside, start permitting him to leave the house. The tom will devote its sprayings to its outside territory. Its indoor spraying will decrease sharply.

If the cat is indoor-outdoor and already fixed, but sprays anyway, clean the area with a special no-spray solution that can be found at most pet supply stores. Then change your cat's association with his favorite spraying spot by moving his feeding station to the area in question. Most cats have a natural aversion to soiling their feeding areas

Begging

When it comes to prying treats from their masters, cats can be appallingly persistent—both in their patient perches and stares, and in their demonstrative mewing that tugs at their owner's heartstrings (as intended). So powerful is a cat's urge to eat tasty morsels that it is difficult to break it of a begging habit once it has been rewarded.

If you're seated for dinner and the cat shows up at your

This is always a no-no!

feet, staring up with big eyes, you should only blame your-self for not dissuading such behavior. If you have given in before, why shouldn't the cat expect you to yield again? It will assume you have granted it permission to beg.

Three methods can end begging:

1) Don't give in to it. Don't even toss it a scrap from the table.
2) When you're ready for your meal, feed your cat in its bowl in a different room, and, if possible, shut the door to your eating area.

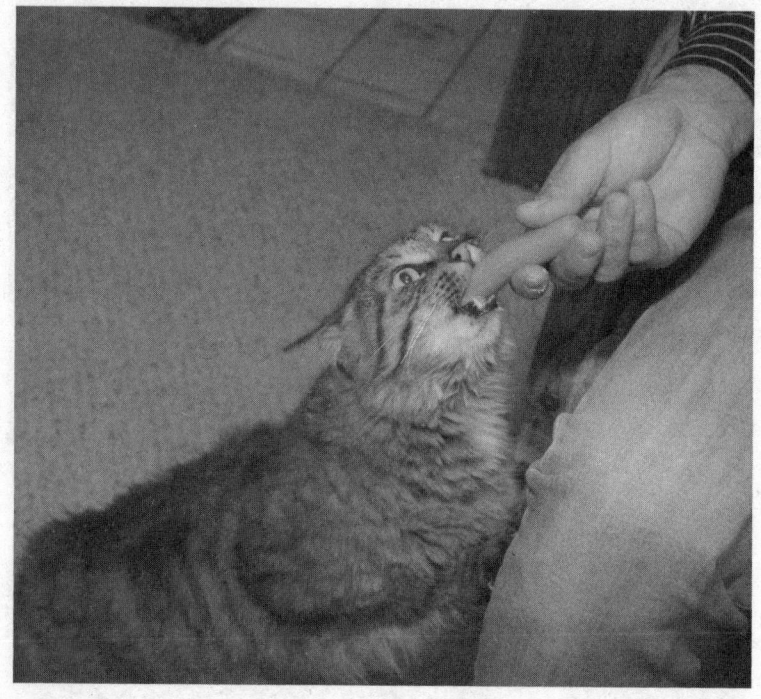

Bad habits are hard to break.

3) Accustom your cat to its eating ritual by adding extra signals—calling it with your voice, or ringing a bell. That will further instill in its mind where it is meant to eat (its bowl), instead of sitting at your feet in the people's dining area.

🐾 PAW PRINTS 🐾

- If you punish a cat for a misdeed, it must be at the scene of the crime and immediately after the transgression—or the cat won't link your scolding words or clapping hands or spritz of water with its action.

Playing Innocent

Cats can play dumb when they want. Some are quite aware that this is a fine ploy to pull on a person if the cat has deliberately violated a taboo of the house but wants to escape punishment.

I was sitting at my computer, working away, when I noticed my cat, Kuza, who was lying on a chair nearby, staring at a piece of bologna left on the kitchen table. My cats are trained from the time they are little kittens not to jump on the table. Each one of them understands this is a cardinal rule in the Popovich house. Kuza is no exception.

Nevertheless, I sensed something was up. My suspicion was heightened after Kuza got up from the chair, walked around, then returned to the chair and lay down. I must note that he is one of my smarter cats. He is a calico with brown, yellow and white spots, and lots of confidence. At the time of this incident, he was about age seven. In other words, more than old enough to know better. (Or, looked at a different way, old enough to be rather wily!)

I returned my focus to the computer screen. From the corner of my eye, I saw Kuza leap up onto the table, grab the bologna, and jump back down. In a flash he was back on the chair, lounging as before, with a blank expression on his face.

I got up and walked over to him. "What are you doing? Why did you do that?"

He looked up at me innocently.

"Stand up," I said.

I nudged him up.

Reluctantly he stood.

(Continued)

There was the piece of bologna that had been hidden under his body.

In the next instant, without further ado, Kuza bolted from the chair and ran off. He knew he'd been caught, and that was his only course of action.

A rather sensible cat, wouldn't you say?

- Since you can't monitor a cat 24/7, deterrents such as double-sided adhesive tape to prevent clawing of a couch will help you break a cat of undesirable behavior.
- Remove temptation whenever possible. If you don't want the cat to jump on the table and get into the food there, don't leave food out after a meal.
- Sometimes, a pet's bad behavior—such as repeatedly scratching to be let out, then scratching to be let in a few moments later—is really just a cry for attention. Spend time every day playing with it, and this annoying attention seeking should vanish.
- A cat that has been neutered or spayed before puberty probably will spray little, if at all. If it already has reached puberty, sterilization will decrease its spraying.
- To prevent your cat begging for food, don't ever give in. Ever. Feed the cat in a separate room, and close the door to your eating area, if possible. Ring a bell or call it when its bowl is being filled, to reinforce its eating ritual.

Part III

Advanced Lessons in Cat Training

13

Cats and Kids Living Together

*"An ordinary kitten will ask more questions
than any five-year-old boy."*
—CARL VAN VECHTEN

M ommy and Daddy, I want a kitty!"
This is a common exclamation from a child, although
it's just as likely that he or she will ask for a puppy or rabbit,
hamster or goldfish. In each case, the reason is the same: No
matter how many toys a child has, or how expensive the toys,
they cannot provide the intimate connection a child enjoys
with a real live pet.

Psychologists say that owners keep household pets for the
emotional support the animals provide. These people may not
receive enough attention or affection from their family; a pet
provides this companionship. In a family, sometimes the lone-
liest person is the child, somewhat lost in the hustle and bustle
of modern living, with two working parents or a harried single

parent. And even if the child has siblings, they won't always get along or be in the mood to play with each other.

A pet provides friendship and attention to the child, and is dependent on the child for its needs, and for once the child is in control with no authority figure involved. The pet will interact with the child and listen to the child's commands or comments without interrupting. The child assumes a much-needed position of importance. What's more, the child learns responsibility. Given the tasks of feeding the pet, grooming the pet, playing with it, seeing to its outdoor needs, and cleaning its litter box, the child develops nurturing skills. And a parent charging the child with these duties makes the child feel like the parent trusts him or her, strengthening the parent-child relationship.

A psychologist was interviewing a four-year-old boy as part of an intelligence assessment.

Psychologist: "So, how many paws does your kitty-cat have?"
Boy: "Four."
Psychologist: "Good. And how many ears does kitty have?"
Boy: "Two."
Psychologist: "And how many eyes does kitty have?"
Boy: "Two."
Psychologist: "And how many tails does kitty have?"
Boy, exasperated: "Mommy, this silly man's never seen a cat before?"

Research has shown that caring for a pet benefits the mental and behavioral growth of a child. And a cat is perfectly suited as a child's pet, provided that the child is old enough and mature enough to tend to the cat's needs. If a child is still very young—say age seven or under—a cat can still be an appropriate pet, but the parent must remain actively involved in supervising the animal's daily care.

From my own childhood experiences, I can say that a cat helps a child develop self-confidence as the youngster learns to build trust with the animal by ensuring the cat's needs are covered, and by behaving in a way that elicits the cat's affectionate behavior. The lessons are many. One is that the child cannot be mean to the cat lest the animal avoid the child and perhaps lash out. The child learns that even though he or she is larger than the cat, pulling the cat's tail or holding the cat too tightly, or against its will, will estrange the cat. If a child neglects to fill the food or water bowl, the cat similarly will withhold its respect and faith.

I mentioned in Chapter Six how, in my circus family, dogs and cats were my closest friends as we traveled from town to town. It wasn't until I was three or so, and had developed some social skills (such as restraint and tuning into other beings' feelings), that Timothy, our pet tomcat, would allow me to reach out and touch him. Up to that point he'd come within a few feet of me, scrutinize me, but not allow me to lay a finger on him—surely sensing that I could seize his tail if given the chance. I also related in Chapter Six that our pet cat Pucha—normally a faithful and playful friend—taught me never to interrupt her meal. Her sharp nip on my wrist as I interrupted her meal one night sent me crying from hurt and betrayal to my mother, who explained to me that Pucha had the same right to eating undisturbed as we did.

. . .

THERE ARE SEVERAL CAVEATS to consider before bringing a cat home for your child. Foremost is whether one of the adults in the house can assume the ultimate responsibility for the pet's welfare, given that the child must learn to care for the animal. The adult must not only instruct the child on how and when to provide the daily food and water for the cat, but to inspect (and clean, if the child is old enough) the litter box, and to regularly check the cat's ears and eyes, teeth, paws, and fur to ensure the cat is in good health, free of illness or injury. And even more basic: The adult must explain from the start that the animal must be treated with kindness and thoughtfulness, gentleness and dignity.

A parent's supervision also is critical since the child can't carry out the more complicated responsibilities such as purchasing the food, litter-box filler, and other necessities, or tend to the larger tasks—installing a pet door, and scheduling and keeping veterinarian appointments.

Here are some other key points to ponder before giving a child a cat:

- A parent must be willing to carefully and thoroughly explain to the child the proper care and treatment of the cat. The child must be taught that he or she and the cat are mutually dependent on each other.
- If a parent dislikes cats, it is a bad idea to bring one into the home, since the parent has to control the relationship between the child and the cat.
- Is there money in the household budget to provide fully for a cat's needs? A cat has special nutritional and health

care needs that must be met so that it can enjoy a healthy, full life, as it deserves.

- Is anyone in the home allergic to cats? It would be deeply disappointing, maybe even devastating, for a child to have to give up its beloved pet because someone in the home is allergic.

The experience of raising and caring for a cat can provide great joy and satisfaction to a young person. The animal will impart many important social lessons, including respect for other beings. But before introducing a new cat to the home, an adult must make sure the child understands the responsibilities that come with having a cat. Once the cat is introduced, the adult should carefully supervise the child and cat to make sure the needs are being met.

IS THERE A PREGNANT woman in the house? She may run the risk of toxoplasmosis. This is a disease caused by an intestinal parasite that infects mammals, such as cats, that eat smaller animals, such as birds, that carry toxoplasmosis cysts. The cysts in the predator's intestines develop into eggs that are shed in feces.

If a pregnant woman is infected, perhaps after cleaning the litter box, the parasite can cause birth defects. The risk of contracting toxoplasmosis can be avoided with simple precautions. One is to assign litter-box cleaning to someone other than the pregnant mother. Another is to have the vet test the cat for illness, then keep the cat indoors so it won't hunt outside and contract the disease.

Cat Care Checklist

The child must be taught that the cat requires daily:

- Nutritious cat food.
- Clean drinking water.
- Quiet time and privacy—in an area set aside specifically for it.
- Playtime with the child.
- Loving attention from the child. (This includes kind words, and also petting. Cats love being stroked over the back and down to the tail base, and around the face and neck.)
- Visits to the veterinarian on the recommended schedule.
- A clean litter box.
- A scratching post.
- Favorite toys.

Here are no-no's in handling the cat:

- Tossing it, or dropping it from a high place. The misconception that cats always land on their feet should be corrected among children interested in trying out this concept. Too long or hard a fall, and the cat can be severely injured or even killed.
- Screaming at or chasing it.
- Moving quickly around it. (The proper way is to move slowly around the cat so as not to surprise or frighten it.)
- Throwing objects at it.
- Allowing friends to tease or play rough with it.
- Yelling at it or otherwise punishing it for a perceived wrong action, such as not using the litter box. (Positive reinforcement is preferred, and much more effective.)
- Pestering a cat that has been overly excited or angered.

 (The animal will need a few hours to cool down.)
- Interrupting its meals or use of the litter box.
- Interrupting its slumber.
- Seizing or hiding its toys.
- Providing it with inappropriate toys or objects that can cut it or it can choke on.
- Pulling its tail.
- Grabbing its ears.
- Petting it too long.
- Stroking its belly.
- Seizing its paws. (Especially not lifting it by its paws.)
- Trying to lift it by grabbing around its middle. Children have small hands and may try this method. But the proper way of lifting a grown cat—provided it will allow you to do this—is to place a palm under its breast while gently clasping the front paws with your fingers, while the other hand supports the back end of the body. This prevents straining of the cat's back. A kitten can be grasped at its nape, but a second hand must support it under the abdomen.

Sadly, some families give up their cats after a woman becomes pregnant. Sometimes it's because the family fears for the safety of the infant they're expecting. A myth that seems bred of fear and superstition, since it is unsubstantiated by actual recorded events, is that a cat, being jealous of a newborn baby capturing a household's attention, will place its nose in a sleeping infant's mouth and suffocate the helpless child. A variation of this is an old wives' tale that a cat will smell milk on the infant's breath and move to the newborn's mouth, sucking out the child's breath.

While it's not out of the realm of possibility that a cat could curl up around a sleeping baby and unintentionally suffocate the child, it seems an extremely remote danger. The vast majority of cats will have no interest in the baby and will avoid it, favoring the adults who feed it and meet its needs. And yet as a precaution, it's best to place the nursery, and especially the crib, off limits to the cat. A cat could lie near a baby's head and expose the baby to allergens and parasites. The cat also might jump on or scratch the baby.

Whenever the cat approaches or enters the baby's room, shoo it away. Keep the door closed whenever possible. And closely monitor all instances when the cat can interact with the infant, and never leave the two alone together.

Since a newcomer to the household will upset some of the cat's usual habits, expect the cat to go through a period of adjustment. It may not use its litter box, it may eat less, or it may perform excessive grooming, until its added stress subsides. You can acclimate your cat to the arrival of a newborn by buying the cat extra toys beforehand, since it will be receiving less human attention in the house. Let the cat sniff the baby's blanket and carrier, and even the child's little toys and face, so it will grow familiar with the scent.

An infant or toddler is not much of a physical risk to a cat, but as the child grows, it's important to teach the youngster not to pull the cat's ears, tail or fur, or to chase it or throw objects at it. "No!" is the key word. Teach the child that the cat deserves respect.

If a cat, in self-defense, scratches or even bites the child, medical care is immediately required. Watch for swelling in the child's lymph glands, which can signify bacterial infection. And if a cat draws blood with its attack, the child should receive antibiotics.

Sebastian.

The cat will adapt to the baby and adjust its habits as the child gains increasing mobility. A child wheeling around in a toddler's chair will prompt the pet to find resting spots out of harm's way—such as atop a dryer or under a bed.

In time, the cat and child will not only cohabit well, but come to love each other.

☙ PAW PRINTS ☙

- No matter how many toys a child has, nothing equals the experience of caring for a pet.
- Children lacking enough attention in the household often ask for a pet. An animal can provide companionship and fulfill other emotional needs of a child,

such as fostering self-esteem and confidence, and teaching responsibility.

- An adult in the household must assume ultimate responsibility for the pet's welfare, even though daily duties are delegated to the child.
- Before giving a cat to a child, consider whether the household budget can sustain a pet, whether the adult supervisor likes cats, and whether anyone in the home is allergic to cats.
- A child must be taught from the start to care for all a cat's daily needs.
- Pregnant women run the risk of toxoplasmosis, a disease that an outdoors cat can transmit from eating smaller animals that carry the parasite. Simple precautions—such as having someone else clean the litter box, testing the cat for illness, and keeping the cat indoors—can remove the risk.
- It is a myth that a cat—out of jealousy, or attracted by the scent of milk—will suffocate a baby. But a cat can irritate or harm a baby by spreading allergens or parasites, or jumping or scratching. Keep a cat out of the nursery, and never leave a cat alone with an infant, unsupervised.
- Teach the young child to respect the cat. Over time, the two will become friends.

14

Bringing an Additional Cat into Your Home

*"If you want to be a psychological novelist and
write about human beings, the best thing you can do
is own a pair of cats."*
—ALDOUS HUXLEY

There are important factors to consider before adding a second cat to your family.

First, do you have the extra time, money, and space to devote to this addition? Second, will the resident cat welcome a companion—or will it deeply resent the intrusion? And third, is your cat sufficiently sociable to get along with a permanent newcomer?

As mentioned in Chapter Two, when acquiring a kitten it's often a good idea to get two at a time. Choose two that seem bonded already (perhaps from the same litter). They'll keep each other company. If you're commonly out of the house for long hours, the kittens will prevent each other from growing bored and lonely. Bringing them home at the same time rather than returning for the second kitten eases the transition to the new household. Kittens are also more open and sociable than adult cats, so they're much more likely to become friends if they meet as kittens.

But if you have a resident adult cat, think carefully before bringing a new cat into the picture. If you decide you can support a new cat and spend the quality time necessary to nurture it, also examine whether your current cat is rather timid—hiding from guests when they arrive, and behaving unsociably toward other animals, including cats. In this case, a new cat may add significant stress to the established cat. Since its welfare is your responsibility, you may decide to forego a second cat.

If a new cat still seems the right choice, know that you will have to manage a period of transition for both animals. The established cat will most likely be jealous of two aspects of the newcomer's appearance in the home:

1) The invasion of its territory, which it now must share.
2) The divided attention it now receives from you, its owner.

A parent of two or more children may well recognize the behavior patterns as like those of an envious older sibling toward a younger one.

Buba and Oogle Come to Terms

Any time a new pet joins the World Famous Popovich Comedy Pet Theater, there is an adjustment period for the entire cast. The newcomer has to struggle to fit in, make a friend or two, and otherwise earn acceptance, or at least tolerance, from the rest of the crew.

The first few days among the other animals can be full of tension. A new animal may be picked on by one or more of the others, but I'll intervene right away, and the other pets will quickly realize that this new arrival is part of the team, and fighting with it is not allowed. The most common scenario is my having to control a dog from chasing a new cat in the house. I'll explain to the dog that this newcomer is our friend. The rules are slightly different outside: In the yard, it's natural for a dog to chase a cat. It's really just a game. But no biting is allowed.

Part of the challenge for the new animal to gain respect from the others stems from jealousy on the part of the veterans. As my assistants and I train the new animal to perform whatever trick the animal displays a knack for and interest in, the other pets resent the time and attention given this stranger. This has led me to exercise caution when I interact with a new addition to our troupe while the others are present. If I walk into a room full of pets and greet the recent arrival with, "Good kitty! Feel comfortable!" and stroke it, while ignoring the other animals, the moment I leave the room, trouble is bound to ensue. To prevent a spat, I make sure to pet and say a few kind words to each and every other animal in the room.

One of the most difficult Comedy Pet Theater veterans to

(Continued)

win over is Oogle, one of the oldest cats in my troupe. ("Oogle" is the Russian word for "night"; he is so named because of his black fur. I will share a story about him in Chapter Sixteen.) Oogle is one of the leaders of the feline corps. At mealtime he goes first to eat, with the other cats respecting his status. If he decides he wants a spot on the couch, he'll jump onto it, and any other cats already there will scatter to make room.

I adopted a gentle brown mongrel dog named Buba. He came to distinguish himself with two entertaining specialties. First, he mastered the stunt of climbing a swing-set ladder and sailing down the slide, repeating the trick again and again. Second, he played well the role of a slow-moving dim-wit, and so I put him in my schoolhouse sketch, and had him sit at a student's desk and not be able to bark an answer when asked to solve an arithmetic question was written on the chalkboard.

It would be hard for anyone not to take a shine to Buba. He is extremely likeable. However, Oogle didn't care much for Buba's immediate popularity among us people.

Oogle took to spraying his territorial mark on Buba's bed mat—right where the poor pooch liked to lay his head. Buba, of course, couldn't sleep on a damp bed; he had to find a different place. I had to clean his sleeping mat again and again in the washing machine. I figured that this rudeness and insecurity on Oogle's part would cease after awhile, as the cat got used to Buba's scent and accepted Buba's membership in our extended family.

Two weeks passed, and Oogle was still acting out. As I was working with Buba one afternoon, his feline nemesis brazenly strode over to the dog's mat and sprayed yet again.

Some time later, about ten minutes before I customarily took the dogs for their daily walk, I began gathering them up from their cages. Buba had something on his mind. He walked over to Oogle's litter box, lifted a hind leg and left his canine calling card. My assistants and I were beside ourselves. Our jaws dropped. We'd witnessed a very humanlike act of retribution.

Buba's statement got its point across. Oogle's insults stopped after that.

It proved to me how intelligent animals can be. A lot more is going on inside their heads than we give them credit for.

HERE IS HOW YOU, the owner, can understand and best manage the arrival of a new cat into the fold:

Keep the new cat in a separate room or portion of the house for the first week. Introduce the cats for a few minutes a day, gradually extending the time they're together.

When introducing the newcomer to the resident cat, do so in an area large enough to allow each animal to maneuver around. Keep an eye on them. If it is necessary to discipline them, should they tangle with each other, it is the older cat you must scold, not the newcomer adjusting to a strange environment.

The established cat, especially if it is older and large, may attack the new cat. If this happens, keep the animals separated in different rooms and only allow them to encounter each other in your presence. Eventually they will grow used to each other, and even get along excellently. This may take place over the course of a week or a few weeks. The key is that during the initial phase of getting to know each other, you must supervise their playtime together. (Typically, they'll sit at a distance from each other, watching each other, without interacting. They're getting used to each other's smells and presence.)

You'll know they've reached a breakthrough in their relationship when they no longer fight. After a year passes, even cats that started off very badly together may end up friends.

If the original cat proves to be overbearing in its behavior toward the younger newcomer, don't grow upset. Know that this is the normal behavior of an adult animal toward a junior, and it is helping the newbie learn its place in the home. A frequent pattern is one in which the adult cat at first completely ignores a kitten brought to the home. Eventually, the elder probably will warm to the younger.

If your cat has been sterilized (as I highly recommend) then its acceptance of the newcomer will be much easier. An unneutered tomcat will aggressively enforce its territorial imperative by repelling any perceived invader.

Some adult cats cannot adjust well to the addition of a new cat. (To grasp the sensitivity of cats to intruders, know that even the scent of a strange cat carried on your clothes can cause displeasure and alarm when your pet cat sniffs the odor.) The first cat's offense at having its space compromised and its owner's attention and affection given to another animal can lead to psychosomatic disorders. The established cat can begin spraying outside its litter box, be in a chronically foul mood, refuse to eat, and stop grooming itself. In extreme cases, it could scratch itself to the point of bleeding, suffer from diarrhea and vomiting, or have its hair fall out. Some breeds, such as Siamese, are ultrasensitive. You may decide it's best to find another home for the newcomer.

While it is difficult not to dote over an adorable kitten, take pains to avoid doing this in the presence of the established cat. It must feel that you are still giving it attention and affection, so that it its resentment of the newcomer is moderated. Lavish the resident cat with attention and affection, which will help ward off jealousy and resentment.

In line with not showing favoritism toward the newcomer, feed both cats at the same time. And to ensure the established cat doesn't feel it's being crowded, set each cat's food and water bowl at opposite ends of a room or even in different rooms. As time goes on, you can soften these rules and eventually consolidate the feeding area. The same is true with litter boxes. Give each one a separate box during this transitional period.

IT IS POSSIBLE THAT the two cats will never become bosom buddies, or even playmates. But there is a good chance that companionship will indeed develop. Although domestic cats are popularly thought to be aloof and prefer solitary lives, in fact they are predisposed to forming groups with fellow cats. In this regard, domestic cats are like their larger cousins, lions.

In the wild, cats will form colonies, and within the colonies will be clusters of same-sex cats. Adult females and their kittens collect together. They are visited during mating season by dominant males, who tend to live on their own and carve out territories. Meanwhile, young adult males band together. These tomcats don't fight much with each other, but instead patrol their area and attack strange cats that enter.

As your first cat and the newcomer grow used to each

other, sharing the same territory under the same roof, a natural bond should develop.

CATS AND OTHER ANIMALS IN THE HOUSE

Can cats cohabit peacefully with household pets of other species?

The answer is yes—under the proper circumstances.

Not surprisingly, a major factor is the cat's individual nature, as well as the personalities and inclinations of the other animals. Of course, animals are predisposed to certain actions; as predators and prey, they are inclined to eat each other, or to avoid being eaten. But there are certain steps you can take if you want a diverse, functional pet family.

(And please keep in mind that if you intend to house animals that, in the wild, would be living out roles dictated by the food chain, it is up to you—entrusted with your pets' care—to ensure each one is safe under your roof. For example, don't let a cat get at a pet bird.)

In general, a cat raised from kittenhood around pets of other species will be much more likely to befriend or tolerate these creatures. Dogs, even older dogs, make friends more easily with other animals than do cats. But a cat that has grown up around other animals will be more receptive to the addition of a new animal later on.

Acquiring your cat and the other pet at the same time boosts the chances for harmonious coexistence even more. And if each pet is young, so that they grow up together, this will ease their introduction to each other.

You must never forget to cater to the animal's natural

needs. Cats are territorial and do not take kindly to what it perceives to be an interloper. So if you bring in a new pet (including another cat), confine the newcomer to a room or section of the home for a few days instead of letting it roam the entire house.

You must realize that animals need to get used to each other—and this should be done gradually. Give your cat the opportunity to sniff the new animal—ideally, when the newcomer is sleeping—so that the cat can familiarize itself with this new housemate, lose its fear or resistance to the unknown, and feel better about sharing its territory. If this isn't possible, allow the animals to sniff bedding or items that the other animal has used.

Supervise the first face-to-face meeting, perhaps with another person present so that each of you can restrain the prospective parties. Be ready to intervene if the chance of violence or a chase seems imminent.

Remember that each animal deserves its security. If the cat is a threat to the other animal, you must provide a living spot protected from the cat's lethal teeth and claws. Similarly, if the cat represents prey to the new animal, make sure the cat has a safe, accessible hiding place in case trouble arises. Moreover, keep a close eye on monitoring the animals when they're in proximity of each other. When you or no other person is home to supervise, make sure the animals are physically separated—such as behind closed doors in separate rooms.

Animal housemates, like their human counterparts, need a period of adjustment in which to get used to each other. If an adult cat is one of the parties, it can take months, and even as long as a year, for boundaries to be defined and mutual respect developed. If disharmony appears, try to wait it out before making any important decisions about keeping both pets under your roof.

TIPS FOR PROMOTING INTER-ANIMAL TRANQUILITY

Dogs

Nature instilled a natural predatory drive in dogs. This drive is higher in some breeds (such as terriers, bred to kill rats) than others (such as border collies, bred to herd livestock). Yet a dog's inclination is to chase and kill smaller animals and eat them.

Training can moderate this drive. If you can bring each animal into the same room and get them used to each other—and avoid a situation where the dog enters prey-chase mode and the cat flees in escape mode—then you will be working toward a happy relationship that respects boundaries.

One effective method is to have another person join you for a series of short acclimation sessions with your dog and cat. Put your dog on a leash and have your accomplice hold your cat on the other side of the room. Although your dog will grow excited at seeing the cat, restrain it, and praise it for remaining in the sit/stay position.

Your friend can carry the cat a few steps closer. As long as the dog doesn't strain and try to reach the cat, praise the dog and continue the exercise. Similarly, give him a loud, "No, leave it alone!" command and jerk the lease sharply back if the dog lunges for the cat. Repeat this brief session over several days—each time bringing the cat closer to the dog.

As with all animal training, patience is key. Your first objective is having the cat share space beside the dog without the dog going after the cat. Your next objective is releasing the dog from your hold and letting it roam the room with the cat present. Be ready to grab its leash and scold it if it initiates a chase. Your final goal is allowing the animals to wander freely in the house without your supervision.

I suggest confining your dog and letting the cat roam the house and yard, familiarizing itself with the dog's scent and accepting it as an occupant of the home. Then confine the cat and allow the dog to sniff the home and yard.

Puppies prove more problematic than adult dogs in learning to live with cats. Puppies are energetic and playful and their romping exuberance is greatly irritating to a cat, compromising its sense of independence and need for space. Merely keeping the two animals physically separated won't bring about the goal of mutual acceptance.

As with an adult dog, the method of introduction and customization of a puppy to a cat must take place gradually. Bringing each into the same room, and rewarding the leashed puppy for not paying attention to the cat, makes for a constructive session. Another good training exercise is putting the cat in a room with the door open, but protected behind a baby gate, so the puppy can observe the cat. Reward the puppy for not barking at or trying to reach the cat.

Once your cat and dog are sharing the home with no hostility, they still need to be monitored. You can help maintain the peace by making sure the cat's food and water bowls and litter box are inaccessible to the dog. Also, police the cat from approaching the dog when it's eating or chewing on a bone.

Rabbits
Pet cats, although programmed as hunters, don't necessarily chase pet rabbits. In fact, sometimes a pet rabbit will chase a

cat. The best way to introduce the two is with the rabbit in its cage (and make sure the wire is woven so that openings are too small for a cat's paw to get through).

The rabbit and cat can get used to each other's sounds, scents, and movements. The cat can observe the rabbit hopping and dashing about. This process of acquaintance can take a few days or even weeks. When you feel the time is right, you can remove the rabbit from its cage and let the two move freely in the room, with you present to supervise. But give the rabbit and cat a chance to work out their differences on their own. As long as the cat doesn't become aggressive, allow it to sniff and take stock of the rabbit.

One possible scenario can surprise you: The rabbit bossing around the cat. Rabbits are group animals, while cats are solitary, and an encounter can trigger the rabbit's instinct to establish a hierarchy. It may bully or charge at the cat. The cat, for its part, may note that this strange furry animal is not running from it, and therefore the cat won't be prompted to go into hunting mode. It may decide that the rabbit isn't worth the trouble, and back off.

The good news is that an assertive rabbit won't continue running at the cat; once satisfied that the pecking order is in place, the rabbit will accept the cat. The two can live in peace from then on.

Birds

Although cats, as natural hunters, are hardwired to stalk and pounce on birds, some cats can distinguish between wild birds and pet birds, and won't bother the latter. But the surest method for keeping your fine, feathered birdies intact is to keep them out of Sylvester's reach. A cage stand can be flimsy and an aggressive cat can topple it over—sending it tumbling to the ground. A cage suspended from the ceiling and at a safe distance from elevated surfaces such as bookshelves is ideal.

Cats are resourceful, to be sure. Conscientiously moving cages into a room with a closed door when you're not home will keep the cat away from the birds.

You also must discipline your cat for any moves it makes toward a bird. A verbal "no" and, if necessary, a spritz from a water pistol or sprayer can train it to quit paying attention to the bird cage.

If yours is an indoor-outdoor cat and you worry about it preying on wild birds—such as those attracted by birdseed—a solution is a bell on the cat's collar as a warning system for the birds.

Hamsters or mice

Unless your cat was raised from kittenhood among these pets, it will never accept these creatures as anything other than a potential meal. So, as with birds, keep your rodents safely protected in their cages. Deter the cat's approaches with verbal reproaches and water squirts. The best scenario is keeping the cages in a room inaccessible to the cat.

Snakes

Mammals and snakes do not mix amicably. A cat can hurt or kill a young snake. A snake, if it's a constrictor, can kill your cat. Snakes are known to escape their cages, so do your best to keep them carefully locked up.

Fish

Your fish swimming in a bowl or aquarium can draw your cat's fixed attention, but not necessarily because the fish look like food to the cat. The motion alone catches its eye. Cats are attracted to moving objects.

Domestic cats evolved in a desert environment and aren't natural fishers, but pet cats have been known to kill pet fish. If you keep pet fish, make sure their containers are out of the cat's reach.

Martina and Francesca

The eight to ten cats in my stage show live in their own special portion of the house. My daughter, Anastasia, wanted a pet cat that would live in the family portion of our house only, and not be a part of our act. And so we found Martina at the animal shelter. She was a gray mix of Persian and some other breed with short ears.

Well, Martina couldn't play very well with our show-biz cats, because she suffered from arthritis in a hind leg. That kept her from being as active as the others, and also put her at a slight risk of being hurt, if the others—not aware of her handicap—acted too rough in the chase games cats play.

We decided that Martina would need a play companion. We bought a Chihuahua puppy, Louie, but he and Martina turned out not to like each other. Each basically ignored the other. So we decided to bring a feline friend home for Martina. We chose a three-month-old Russian blue kitten with long hair and nice big eyes. We named her Francesca because of her princesslike bearing. Martina's reaction? Jealousy. I expected as much.

Whenever I've brought a new kitten home from an animal shelter, intending to train it for Comedy Pet Theater, it would be somewhat ostracized by the other cats. As weeks pass, this kitten would make one or two friends among the established troupe members. The process of acceptance by the group usually takes about six months.

It's been four months now, as I write this, since Francesca joined our family. I'm confident that in a few more months, Martina will warm to her, and they can be play buddies. But if not, they will just have to coexist. Not every animal is sociable. Some simply prefer their own company, just like some people. But I have a feeling Martina's icy treatment toward Francesca eventually will melt.

After I made the customary introductions with Martina, the older cat made a big show of ignoring the pretty little kitten. That evening I fed each one separately. I put Francesca in a room near the kitchen and closed the door, then walked off to my library.

When I returned a few minutes later, I stopped in my tracks because of an amusing sight. Martina left her bowl and stalked over to the door, bent down, and attempted to peer underneath the door to scope out the newcomer.

The moment I entered the room and Martina saw me, she rose and ran away, sending the nonverbal message: *No, I'm not interested.*

Cats can lie, of course. Just like people.

❧ PAW PRINTS ❧

- Before acquiring a second cat, consider if you have the money, space, and time to devote to it.
- Supervise the introduction of the cats to each other. The first cat may ignore the second, but it also may attack it. Don't be alarmed if the first cat is overbearing toward the younger addition: It's teaching the newbie its place.
- A sterilized cat will welcome a newcomer more easily. An unneutered tomcat, especially, will enforce its territorial against a perceived invader.
- Some adult cats can't adjust to the sudden intrusion into their territory of a newcomer and the attention from the owner the newbie commands. In extreme cases, the first cat can suffer psychosomatic illnesses.
- Take pains not to ignore the first cat and dote over the second when the cats are together. That will only increase the first cat's jealousy. Show the resident cat how important it is by lavishing it with love and attention.
- Cats and dogs in the same home can learn to coexist. So can cats and rabbits, and even cats and birds.
- Cats are predisposed to associating with members of its species. In the wild, they form colonies. So chances are that two cats in a household will bond.

15

Moving to a New Home

"A cat has too much spirit to have no heart."
—ERNEST MENAULT

Moving is one of the most stressful experiences for people. It takes a toll on pets, too. When a cat changes homes, it's like losing a piece of itself. It has been torn away from its familiar territory and all its cherished routines.

Unlike people, who mentally prepare for the move, the cat's uprooting takes it completely by surprise. Now it's bombarded by all the sights, sounds, and smells of a strange new environment. And its owner's agitation in managing and carrying out the move affects the cat, that most sensitive of creatures. It, too, will feel nervous and unsettled, and will want to return to the place it still considers home—the old house.

A cat that has been allowed to roam outdoors will survive the move better and recover quicker than a cat that has been indoors only, because a cat used to exploring the outdoors is accustomed to encountering new environments with their strange, different sensory delights and set of dangers. But at the same time, a cat used to the outdoors is more prone to try to escape the walls of the new home and find its way back to the old.

The period of adjustment to the new place, so that the cat understands it is the permanent home, commonly takes about a month. Your tasks in helping your cat adapt are two-fold:

1) Get it used to the new home so that it feels comfortable and secure there.
2) Keep it from escaping the home during this transitional period.

A GOOD STRATEGY FOR moving is setting up your new home—furniture and all—before bringing your pets over. Either have someone babysit the pet at a different home, or keep the cat behind a closed door in the old home so that it doesn't get lost or trampled underfoot during the move, or escape the home (a high-risk time for this to occur). A cat that sees the familiar furniture missing, and boxes and rolled-up carpets suddenly appearing will freak out; better that the animal be confined to a separate room.

When you finally do bring your cat over, make sure it has a sturdy carrier and that the carrier is closed properly. As you carry the cat to and from the car, and during the journey, talk as gently as possible to it as it is probably extremely anxious. It may be meowing loudly. At the new house, have a quiet room set up with its familiar objects: toys, blankets and scratching post, bowls and litter box. You may even leave a blanket or shirt with the old home smell on it in the room with the cat. It's a good idea to make sure your cat is hungry before the move. If it hasn't eaten for 12 hours, its primary concern upon arrival at the new home is eating. Its bowls will be filled with food and water in the special room that is set up for it.

Visit the room from time to time and speak soothingly and reassuringly to your cat. It will be very stressed out for several days. It may decide to hide under a bed or other object for a number of days, coming out only to eat or use the litter box. If your cat seems especially nervous during the move to a new home, consider giving it a calming natural remedy for pets. Brands include Content-UM, Pet Calm, and Rescue Remedy. This may temporarily reduce its anxiety.

When you decide, perhaps on the day following the move, to acquaint the cat with the new environment, know that the unfamiliarity will be overwhelming. You will be its guide. Take it to each room, one by one, and let it explore. Speak kindly and calmly to it. Your gentle tone will help soothe its fear.

Within a day or a two, leave the room's door open. The cat may decide to come out of the room on its own to explore. If you can arrange the furniture in the new home somewhat in the order of the previous home's, so much the better. It will ease the cat's transition even more.

If the home is large, consider returning the cat to the room if you need to leave the house. In its own time, the cat will begin roaming the house, growing familiar with it more intimately than its owners are.

. . .

IF IT HAS BEEN an indoor-outdoor cat, consider keeping it inside for at least two weeks. If your cat does get outside during this transitional period, it may try to find its way back to your old home. If it was an indoor-outdoor cat, it may recognize familiar paths, provided that the new home is not far away from the old. Sometimes a distance of five miles does not deter a cat from traveling back to the old place.

Beyond the perils of dogs and other cats, coyotes and cars, and poisons such as automobile antifreeze, there is a special danger for a cat that undergoes an odyssey of return to the old home. If the cat makes it back to the former residence, it will be astonished at the changes that have occurred. This will confuse it greatly. If its connection to the new home still isn't firm, the cat simply won't be able to recall it now lives there. Suddenly, the animal is in limbo.

If your new home is in fairly close proximity to the old home, it's wise to warn the new occupants of your former home that your cat may try to return. However, if you're moving out of an apartment or other rented home, you may not have this opportunity to meet the new residents.

All the more reason to keep a close eye on your cat for the first month after moving. When you do let your cat out of the new home for the first time, make sure it hasn't eaten for awhile, so that it will feel even more strongly the urge to return inside. On this first foray outside, accompany it. And from that time on throughout the next two weeks, don't feed your cat before letting it out. Give it a half hour or so alone before calling it in. When it arrives, feed it immediately.

Make sure your cat has a way to get back into the new home by itself. If you've had a pet door installed, acquaint the cat with it. If there is no other access than a door to the house, make sure the door stays open for the first few weeks when the cat explores outside. It will be encountering other cats and animals in the neighborhood, and even if your cat is not one to look for trouble, it may end up being attacked or pursued, and need a retreat route.

If your cat does try running away, and it seems apparent it hasn't accepted the new home as its own, you can try this method of weakening its recollections of the former home: Bring it for an extended stay of several days at a friend's or relative's home. When you return the cat to your home, with its familiar smells and sights, it will recognize it better as its own home turf.

All the steps in teaching the cat to call your new home its home involve instilling the understanding that the new home is where the cat is fed and protected, and where its providers live.

❧ PAW PRINTS ❧

- Moving is stressful to pets as well as people. Know that your cat will need a period of adjustment to the new home, perhaps as long as a month.
- Keep your cat confined to a room or have it babysat while the move is taking place.
- The cat is the last thing packed for the move. Transport it in a sturdy carrier and speak gently to it on the journey.
- Confine the cat to a special room set up for it after the transition to the new home. The room will contain the cat's bowls and other necessities, plus items bearing smells from the old home.
- Make sure the cat hasn't eaten for many hours before

the move. It will eat for the first time in the new room, and bond more quickly with the new home.

- The cat may hide under a bed or other object for the first few days. Accompany it on a tour of the home, letting it familiarize itself gradually.
- An indoor-outdoor cat may try to return to the old home, especially if that home is five miles or less away. Don't let such a cat outside for at least two weeks. Accompany it on its first foray outside. Make sure it always has an escape route back into the home.

16

Traveling with Your Cat

"I can't decide if I have a cat or a cat has me."
—ESTHER MARTON

I was the first person ever to train domestic cats for the stage. Early on during this endeavor, as my reputation for performing an act called "Cat Skills" began circulating in the world of show business, I received a phone call from a promoter in Los Angeles.

"Gregory, I hear you have cats in your show. How many cats?"

"Six cats, sir," I said.

He was very interested in hiring me for an engagement at a theater in Southern California. He offered a most handsome fee. I concealed my surprise and we came to terms.

A day before I was to set off from home for the show in California, the promoter called to inquire about my travel plans. He was arranging for accommodations at his end to house my animals and me. "What are you driving down in?" he asked.

"I have a Ford Escort," I said.

"Really? How do you transport the cats?" he asked.

"Oh, I put all six cats in the back seat," I said.

He couldn't believe his ears. Upon further questioning, he realized that the "cats" in my show were housecats—not the trained lions and tigers he'd imagined. Who could blame him for this mistake? The use of domestic cats in a show was a novelty I was pioneering, so the assumption on his part that "cats" meant great cats was entirely understandable.

The promoter was beside himself. He screamed. He yelled. Here he'd advertised a show featuring large, magnificent beasts as one of the acts, and now he was in a real bind. What would the crowd think? And it was too late to do anything about it.

When I showed up at the designated site, I met with the promoter. "Look, my English isn't good enough," I said. "You mentioned cats, and I say, 'Yes, cats.' It's not dogs."

Well, "the show must go on," as the old saying goes. And so the promoter began thinking fast. He hit upon an idea. He had some fake fur material bought from a store, and we assembled little manes on my cats.

Before my act hit the stage, the master of ceremonies announced, "Ladies and gentleman, I must warn you that for the very first time, the cats in our next act will be performing on stage without a protective barrier set up between you and them. Please remain quiet and still. Don't get up and move. Don't shout. Don't even talk."

A nervous hush descended on the theater. I walked onstage carrying a suitcase. I set it down and opened it. Out popped my six cats with their little manes.

The exclamations of surprise and hilarity from the audience, fueled by relief, were deafening.

My cats ran through their routines, the show attendees were highly pleased by seeing how well housecats can perform, and afterward the promoter was happy.

"OK, Gregory, the audience was happy, I don't have any complaints. You got your check."

News of this show spread quickly among promoters and agents. From then on, whenever I spoke with agents or promoters about booking my act, they knew to inquire whether "cats" meant big cats or housecats.

Domestic cats had now arrived in the world of entertainment. I still feel a twinge of pride, knowing I contributed a new element to this industry.

OVER THE YEARS, I've been fortunate enough to crisscross the country with the World Famous Popovich Comedy Pet Theater and perform extensively abroad in 25 nations. As a result, my cats are seasoned travelers—real road warriors. Even when my stage show is appearing in my regular afternoon slot at the V Theater inside the Miracle Mile Shops, in Las Vegas, my 16 trained cats (and 13 dogs and 13 ferrets, white mice, geese and doves) must make the short trip to the Las Vegas Strip in their traveling cages.

In the early years, when my act was performing at Circus Circus in Las Vegas, and later in Branson, Missouri, the act was much smaller and a car was all that was needed to transport our four-legged troupe members. Now a trailer is needed. And for those foreign engagements in Europe or Japan, the pets must endure the rigors of air travel. They hold up well, though. My wife, daughter, and I have grown wise in the ways of organizing pet travel with as little stress and bother as possible.

While my furry wards are very accustomed to and comfortable with traveling, which they have done from tender ages, your cat probably dislikes being taken out of its home environment. The cat may associate the appearance of its travel container to a visit to the veterinarian—not a pleasant occurrence for it. Maybe it remembers

Sugar and Sebastian.

being carried off to a new home in the container, or to be babysat in a strange home.

In any event, a cat's nature is that of a homebody. It dislikes being removed from its familiar environment. It is deeply attached to its home territory. But there are times when it must be transported elsewhere—to the vet's, to a cat show, to a babysitter's, to a vacation destination with the family, to a new home, and so on.

There is a wide variety of travel items available for cats. For short jaunts there are leashes, strollers, and pouch carriers. For longer journeys there are tote baskets, duffel bags, cabins (with mesh walls and portholes), cagelike crates, and cargo carriers. At the lowest end—and good for short car trips—are cardboard carrying boxes with handles and air holes. For air travel, you will need a pet pack or wire crate that is secure and cleared by the airline. If you don't own or care to purchase such a container, airlines usually can provide these carriers for an added fee.

With proper preparation, you can help your cat travel short or even very long distances with minimal hassle and discomfort.

THE SIMPLEST TRIP you can take with your cat is going for a walk. On a leash. That's right—dogs aren't the only pets that get to go for "walkies."

Yes, cats are very independent—and, to tell the truth, some never accept the cat leash as a desirable object. Even cats grown accustomed to leashes don't exhibit anything resembling the exuberance of a dog that catches sight of the leash and is raring to go for an excursion with master. But a leash is useful for a cat owner taking the pet on vacation and needing to give it exercise in a strange environment. A leash also permits the cautious cat owner to engage in regular walks in a crowded city or another complex or inhospitable environment where controlling the pet's movements is desirable. A walk in the park with a leashed cat means not worrying about it suddenly chasing after its first sight of prey—or fleeing at the approach of a strange dog.

Cat leashes come in both a standard model of five to six feet in length, and as a retractable model that allows you to adjust the desired length. (Some retractable models will reel in the cat with the push of a button.) An extra consideration is whether to buy a harness to work with the leash, rather than using a collar. Since cats can squirm out of all kinds of restraints, including collars, a harness is advisable. The harness wraps around the cat's torso; some high-end harnesses resemble padded vests. If you use a collar rather than a harness, make sure the collar is not too tight or abrasive. I prefer leather collars.

As with all cat training, if it begins in kittenhood, the adaptation goes much smoother. A kitten is old enough to be harnessed for a short stroll at two months. Your first use of a harness should be without a leash. Let the cat get used to it indoors. After a few days, attach the leash and tug it to get the cat's attention. The cat eventually will get used to this idea and not mind being tugged so much. However, it's best to tug the cat as little as possible.

Your first outdoor trips with the leash should be brief. And remember that use of the leash should be an enjoyable experience, like a game. Never drag the cat along. A caring cat owner is an affectionate leash user.

THE MOST IMPORTANT RULE when taking a cat in your car is to confine it to a container from which it cannot escape. If a cat can work its head through an opening, that means it can wriggle the rest of itself out (cats don't have collarbones). A cat free to move in a car can prove dangerous, and even fatal, to the occupants. Any source of fright—such as a sudden stop, a car horn or siren—can send the animal, claws exposed, clinging to any ready object, including the driver's head. An anxious cat typically seeks the floorboards of a moving vehicle; imagine if the cat gets between the driver's feet and the floor pedals. The results could be catastrophic.

The container for the cat should be sturdy, spacious enough for the cat to move around in a bit, well-ventilated to receive fresh air, and feature slits for seeing out. A variety of travel containers are available from pet-supply outlets. These range from sturdy cardboard boxes to expensive transport containers that protect the cat from unnerving jolts and frightening sounds. Some of these are metal crates. Soft-sided carriers are produced for in-cabin use on airplanes. These carriers can be cloaked with a warm cover in foul weather, and provide shade in hot weather. Soft warm bedding can be placed on the floors.

Whatever container you choose, ensure that when traveling it isn't baking in sunlight. If the temperature in the car is hot because air-conditioning isn't available, keep a spray bottle handy to spritz the cat's face and paws. The cat won't like this, but the water will keep it from getting overheated. And make sure you never leave your cat in a parked car, which can quickly become sweltering and cause inhumane conditions.

When traveling with your cat, a favorite blanket and toy can be set inside the container as creature comforts. A cat displeased with being in the box and in a moving car may cry loud and long; just know that if the trip is lengthy, the cat eventually will calm down and perhaps even snooze. If the trip is to last long, ensure that food and water are in the container. A shoebox with litter filler will be a necessary addition to the container.

To acclimate a cat to car trips, get it used to its carrying box beforehand. At home, place the cat in the box and even let it sleep in it. Later, put the cat in the box and place it in the parked car so that it gets used to this situation. Eventually you can start the motor, so that the cat grows accustomed to the sounds and vibrations. After a few minutes, shut off the motor and carry the container back inside the home. You can repeat this exercise a few times before taking your cat on an actual trip.

CATS ACTUALLY TRAVEL BETTER by air than in automobiles. You'll need to check with the airline beforehand to see whether it allows pet cats to travel with owners in the cabin. If not, the cat will be traveling in the cargo hold. There will be rules for what kind of cat carriers are permitted. You can purchase such a container or, in some cases, rent one from the airline. The best containers I've found are made of durable plastic with metal doors, specifically designed for air travel.

Airlines also have regulations about pet tranquilizers. You always should consult your veterinarian on whether you should administer a tranquilizer to your traveling pet. The same is true for traveling by rail. You'll need to check with the railway company on its regulations for allowing cats to travel with their owners in the rail cars. As with flying, travel by rail is less stressful on cats than car travel, as long as the trip isn't too long.

Whatever the mode of transport, a cat should not be confined longer than 24 hours in a row in a travel container. The cat must be given the chance to get out, stretch and walk. And you will want to replenish its food and water and clean its litter box.

The removal of a cat that has been cooped up in a travel container for many hours on end is a situation in which the cat leash is crucial to happy traveling. A cat already uncomfortable and agitated because of being confined is not a merry soul to begin with. Even in the best of circumstances, all

sorts of disturbances can frighten a cat in this state of mind—
and send it rushing out of its owner's arms.

It's difficult enough adhering to a tight travel schedule.
Hunting down a scampering, hiding cat is not a desirable
situation for either party.

Snow Skips out on the Vet

Here's proof that cats never forget a bad experience.
In this regard, their memories are infallible.

As I mentioned in the introduction, the first cat I adopted
in America was Snow, the all-white beauty I found in an animal shelter in Las Vegas. This year-old cat would complete
our household and help my wife, daughter and I more quickly
feel comfortable in our new apartment in America.

I dutifully brought Snow to the veterinarian for a checkup
and to receive her shots. As the vet tried administering a ra-
bies inoculation, Snow grew very agitated. Her little body
struggled mightily, and she meowed in loud and violent protest. It took two people to hold her so that the vet could insert
the syringe needle. Snow was so wound up that the vet gave
her a sedative pill.

It occurred to me that as a kitten she must have had a bad
experience with a vet. Her memories enslaved her.

Three months later, while in Trenton, New Jersey, during
a tour with a traveling circus, I brought Snow to a vet so she
could receive her next series of shots. The vet's office was
about four blocks from the grounds where circus tents were
set up. I parked near the front door. I reached down and
picked up Snow's box. I opened the top to check on her, and

(Continued)

she immediately figured out what was up. She picked up scents coming from the vet's office.

She bolted from my grasp, leaped out an open window and scampered off.

I chased after her. She vanished. I called for her. To no avail.

I drove around the block and surrounding streets, over and over, but there was no sign of Snow.

Heartbroken, I drove to the city's animal-control shelter and reported my cat missing. Then I returned to the circus grounds.

And who should show up underneath our motor home? Snow meowed and popped her head out as my wife and I got out of the car.

I can only guess how our cat had found her way back to us in a strange city. Circuses have plenty of pungent smells—from elephants and tigers to cotton candy. Snow must have detected these odors even from several blocks away, and followed her nose.

Ever since that day, I take extra precautions in bringing Snow for her yearly vet visit. I give her sedative pills and put her in her cage. I don't open the cage again until I'm in the vet's office.

Her reaction is much more extreme than my other cats, and hopefully than your cat, too.

TRAVEL NECESSITIES

Whether you're transporting your cat on a short trip across town, such as to the cat sitter or the veterinarian's, or bringing it with you on a long journey, there are several precautions to take.

In general, you need to pack sufficient pet supplies, rather than relying on what you might find along the way or at your destination. You also must maintain a positive and nonchalant attitude around your cat during the journey. It will sense your stress, so remain calm around it. Don't act as if the trip is an extraordinary adventure; the cat should get the impression it's a normal activity, and nothing to continually meow about.

Tips for making the trip easier:

Feeding
Don't give your cat any food for twelve hours before a long trip. That decreases the dangers of it defecating or vomiting out of anxiety or motion sickness.

If the trip will be lengthy, passing through customary meal times, you can feed the cat periodically. If the weather is hot and the temperature is high in the vehicle, provide the cat with water and sufficient ventilation. A bowl full of ice cubes can keep the cat cool when the mercury is soaring.

Carrier stability
As mentioned earlier a cat must never be allowed to wander freely in a car. A proper carrier ensures that the cat can feel support under its feet and will not shift or fall. Neglect this precaution, and you will cause the cat unnecessary fear. And the minute it finds itself able to escape from the container, it could very well race at top speed for a place to hide—and woe to those who happen to be in its claw-exposed path.

Carrier livability
Always ensure your cat can move around in the container, has sufficient airflow, and is not overly exposed to sunlight.

An observation slit—especially during a car ride—will make the cat feel more comfortable. As mentioned earlier, there should be no opening that will allow the cat to push its head through. If it can fit its head through—its entire body can squeeze out.

Home away from home

When you go on vacation to a summer home or cabin or rented condo or other lodging, know that for a cat it's like moving to a new home. It may not adjust to the new environment, even after several weeks. The cat may display health woes such as vomiting and diarrhea. These can be symptoms of homesickness.

Consider sparing your cat this memory. Ask a friend, family member, or neighbor to look after your cat for you while you're away. If you find such a babysitter, leave detailed instructions on the cat's feeding times, favorite toys, outdoor routine, veterinary information, and your contact numbers.

If you're taking the cat with you for an extended stay at a vacation home or other long-term residence, make sure to bring along not only the cat's necessities—food bowls and ample supply of food; litter box and sufficient supply of filler, scooper, and litter-disposal bags; scratching post and bedding—but familiar toys.

Since the cat will feel very disoriented for the first few days, provide it more attention than usual, caressing it and speaking kindly to it. And never let it roam outside by itself.

A long road trip

If you will be stopping at hotels, motels or other lodging accommodations along the way, make sure these establishments allow pets. Plan your itinerary accordingly.

A lengthy car trip of several hundred miles or more is not the time to find out whether your cat is a stalwart road traveler. Acclimate your cat to road conditions beforehand. Take your cat on short drives and make them fun by giving it treats at the end.

If you're going on an extended trip, make sure the cat's shots are current and that you are bringing its proof of vaccination and health certificate with you. Some states require these of pet owners passing through. Also see that your cat's ID tag on its collar is secure. Since your cat will feel even more cooped up than you in the car, bring along its leash for walks outside the car during rest stops.

Before leaving on an extended trip, ask your veterinarian whether he or she recommends a mild pet tranquilizer if your cat is particularly anxious about traveling. Never administer tranquilizers without consulting first with a vet. Often, tranquilizers are unnecessary for traveling cats.

Passage on trains or planes

Always check beforehand with the train company or airline on regulations for transporting pets. And if you'll be crossing international borders, you must know whether vaccinations or quarantines are required, and other regulations related to the transporting and importing of animals.

The good news about train travel is that unless the journey is very long, it's less stressful on cats than car travel.

Air travel can be trying on cats, given the roar of the engines. Air travel is not advisable for pregnant cats. Some airlines refuse to transport young kittens.

As for administering tranquilizers—check with the airline for its regulations, and check, too, with your veterinarian beforehand.

Oogle Gives Gregory a Scare

In the early years of developing my pet act, before I moved into regular residency at the V Theater in the Miracle Mile Mall at Planet Hollywood Resort & Casino, on the Las Vegas Strip, I frequently took my show on the road.

During one period I joined up with the Shrine Circus, crisscrossing the country in my motor home. I had six cats at that point. They stayed in cages set toward the back of the motor home. My wife and our toddler daughter and I logged endless hours driving. This was especially hard for me, because I had come from the Great Moscow Circus, and after that the Ringling Bros. and Barnum & Bailey Circus, where you travel on trains and sleep in train cabins or hotels instead of being behind the wheel yourself and looking after your own sleeping arrangements. I had to get used to driving long distances. I felt like more of a driver than a circus performer! I was glad to have the circus work, of course, but the traveling was wearing me out.

On one trek in Pennsylvania I pulled into a rest area at dusk. We were in the middle of nowhere, out in a forested area. It was autumn, and damp. My family got out and stretched. I opened up the doors of the motor home to air it out. I blinked my eyes and savored the fresh air. Then I spied a black cat darting around the motor home. Oh no! It looked like Oogle, one of my cats. (I mentioned him in Chapter Fourteen. Oogle means "night" in Russian.) How did he get out of his cage?

I raced back and looked into the motor home. The cat cage was open!

I hurried back to where I'd seen my cat. I saw the dark form at a distance. I called to him.

He looked up briefly, then moved off.

I pursued him, beckoning him to return. To my surprise, he didn't listen to me. Instead, he kept walking along, navigating the wet muddy grass and brush. I was flabbergasted about being ignored. I grew more apprehensive as I tailed him down a trail. He continued along through the trees. What had gotten into him? What strange urge was drawing him forth through these unfamiliar woods?

I walked faster but couldn't close the distance. He just wouldn't stop. He kept going. I began feeling despair. How could my beloved pet run away just like this? And what would become of him if I couldn't retrieve him? Besides being a beloved pet, Oogle was one of my prized performers. He was key to my stage act.

I heard the honk of our motor home's horn. My wife was summoning me. We had to stick to a schedule to make it to the next town on time. Deeply discouraged, I walked back.

"I cannot find Oogle," I told my wife. "He ran away!"

She shot me a puzzled look. "He's here," she said.

I walked to the rear of the motor home and stared inside at the cage. Indeed, there was Oogle, right where he belonged!

Thus I absorbed a lesson: Don't try looking for a black cat in a dark room. Your mind can play tricks on you.

What was the poor creature I'd pursued through the Pennsylvania forest? Maybe a marmot, skunk, or other wild animal. Or maybe some other black cat—perhaps wondering why it was being chased.

Cats, of course, may frequently wonder at the folly of humans. But they never tell.

🐾 PAW PRINTS 🐾

- Cats are homebodies by nature and dislike being taken on trips. But a variety of cat products, from leashes to strollers to travel containers, are designed to make cat travel easier.
- Cats as young as two months old can begin learning to use a leash. Acclimate the animal slowly by getting it used to its leash and collar or harness before taking it outside for a short jaunt. Never drag the cat along; make the walk a game.
- The Number one rule for a cat traveling in a car is to make sure it's secure in its container and can't escape.
- A travel container should include creature comforts such as a blanket and a favorite toy. For longer trips, food, water, and a shoebox with litter filler are necessary.
- Airlines and railways have regulations governing cat travel.
- Consult a veterinarian before considering administering cat tranquilizers for travel.
- A cat should not be confined longer than 24 hours in a row in a travel container.

17

Training Your Cat to Do Tricks

*"Perhaps it is because cats do not live by human patterns,
do not fit themselves into prescribed behavior,
that they are so united to creative people."*
—ANDRE NORTON

Teaching your cat to perform tricks on your command can be a healthy pastime for each of you. It's a way to spend time together, bonding. The cat engaged in learning a trick will enjoy the attention you give it, and also benefit from the exercise. It will be an interesting exercise for you, too—testing your patience, to be sure, but proving to be fascinating as you discover your pet's memory abilities.

As long as you don't nurture unrealistic expectations, you will probably find that training your cat to do tricks can be quite rewarding. Cats are amazing athletes. From a crouch, a cat can jump four or five times its height.

The Number One rule to understand beforehand is that

you can only train a cat to do a trick if it involves a behavioral habit it naturally exhibits anyway.

If your cat is a climber, or a retriever, or a jumper, or likes to walk between your feet, you need to design a game based around this behavior. Your objective is twofold:

1) Training the cat to carry on this pattern longer and more athletically than normal.
2) Training it to perform the routine on your verbal and physical cue (such as the order, "Jump!" accompanied by a point of the finger) in front of an audience—meaning, in an environment that may be full of bright lights and loud sounds. (In my case, this is on a full production stage in a theater full of clapping, cheering tourists.)

As painstaking as the process is in practicing with a cat month after month until its physical stunt is perfected and becomes second nature to it, I must say that the other part of the equation—getting the cat to perform when you want it to, instead of only when it feels like it—is more difficult. Any cat owner will appreciate this reality. Consider it a fantastic accomplishment, indeed, when your little furry friend is so trusting of you, and so interested in receiving praise from you, that it will hop through a hoop upon your request. And if it declines your solicitation? Well, no hard feelings, you know.

The Number Two rule to understand is that a cat performs only when it wants to, not just because you want it to.

A cat's mood at any given moment can be affected by a variety of factors, just like a person's. What's more, punishing a cat for not performing is not only cruel but also utterly ineffective. The cat won't connect its lack of interest in engaging in your little game to your sudden use of thunderous language and a swat on its backside. It will only feel that you are being mean. And since cats never forget a negative experience, your cat may decide that playing at all with you is risky business, and begin steering clear of you whenever you show up with a ball or arrange chairs at a jumping distance.

Your aim must be to try and get your cat into the proper mood for performing. This took me a long time, with plenty of trial and error, before I had some breakthroughs in fathoming this area of cat psychology.

Expect the Unexpected with Cats

When I first began training intensively with cats, developing my "Cat Skills" act, I covered every possible scenario I could think of. I acclimated each cat to the stage environment. Not only did I painstakingly play with each cat separately, using a game of performance and reward as I taught it to leap through a hoop or walk a tightrope or do whatever it naturally was inclined to do, but I slowly added more external stimuli to the play area. I'd have my assistants stand nearby and clap or cheer loudly. I'd crank up loud music. I'd shine bright lights on the play area. I'd get the cat very used to carrying out its little trick despite these distractions.

Well, there I was on the Midway at Circus Circus one fine afternoon, confidently conducting my act to hearty applause, feeling the warm elation of pleasing an audience that we stage performers never tire of, and always are grateful for.

(Continued)

Suddenly, there was a loud clanging of bells and a siren sound and a woman whooping with frenzied glee. Someone in the adjacent casino had hit a slot-machine jackpot.

This eruption of excitement spread immediately in the casino, and also turned heads on the Midway. Including on stage. All my cats swung their heads toward the source of the excitement.

It seemed like forever before I could restore order and resume my act. Fortunately, this was one of those occasions that are naturally invested with humor. The crowd appreciated the cats' interest in the jackpot, and laughed along with me (although, indeed, my laughter was rather of the nervous sort).

The moral of this little vignette is that cats, like people, are not machines. You can't expect them always to perform. The unexpected, after all, is a variable, too.

IN THE EARLY STAGES of developing my "Cat Skills" act, while I was still just one in a rotating cast of performers on the Midway at Circus Circus in Las Vegas, I was able to get my cats to accomplish their tricks consistently at my home. I was gratified when they performed the stunts to perfection during rehearsal on stage, responding alertly and with precision to my commands as production music blared and lights glared. But when a real live audience was seated? Never mind the raucous background score and the blazing multicolored stage bulbs. It was the presence of all those people seated before the stage that proved to be a major distraction.

My cats quit paying attention to me, and stared out at all those faces and bodies in the rows of seats.

I was disappointed, but having grown up in the circus world, I was prepared with a backup. When my exhortations, "OK, cat, jump, jump," did not get one of my little sidekicks to spring through the hoop I held, I turned to the crowd, said, "Sorry, guys," and transitioned quickly into a juggling trick (with balls, not with the cats, although a part of me was tempted!).

That's how I learned the hard way that a cat better be very willing to carry out its trick or you'll be standing there forever trying to cajole it into obeying.

How to get inside a cat's mind to instill it with this desire? I discovered that a cat's values are different from a dog's. A dog will go through all sorts of contortions in order to gain a doggy treat. A cat? Well, some do respond regularly to a cat treat as a reward. But most cats—if you have a good connection with them—prefer a loving pat or a little kiss on its cheek from their master, accompanied by an exclamation of praise, such as, "What a good kitty you are!"

The human voice, when used correctly, can have a hypnotizing effect on a cat. It doesn't even matter what you say (cats having very limited vocabularies with human language). What matters is the tone you use. A soft, gentle, affectionate stream of words, resonant, almost humming, in a loving timbre is nearly irresistible to your cat. It lulls it into contentment. As a means of reward, these sweet vocalizations are truly effective.

The greatest secret I learned was to reward my performing cats with grand gestures of affection only *after* they performed their tricks. When rehearsing at home, if a cat hopped through a hoop, that's when I'd give it a generous stroke of

Gregory and friends in a training session.

adoration and sweet words of praise. Don't get the wrong idea. I always speak kindly to my wards and treat them with the utmost dignity and respect. And never would I withhold their essential needs—food, playtime, a clean environment— in order to force them into performing so they could enjoy these amenities and necessities. (A cat, by the way, would reject such servitude in the first place!) But I never showered the cat with effusive displays of gratitude except during our training exercises.

The positive results I enjoyed from this method taught me that a happy cat strives to please its owner, and gains great satisfaction from bringing its owner joy. It is much like the gratification a child gains from doing its parent proud.

Here is another secret about cats, based on my long and involved experience with them. When the relationship is close with its master, the cat has a strong desire to do some-thing to make its master happy. Unfortunately, the cat doesn't know exactly how to go about accomplishing this. But when it is presented a game to play with its master—and the master clearly becomes very happy when the cat performs a certain physical stunt—well, then, the cat feels very glad about the opportunity to bring its master this joy. And the outcome provides a bonus for the cat, of course. It receives adulation, as well.

For me, there was one great advantage to not having to use food treats to bribe a cat into performing a trick. In my act, a number of cats sit on their perches, and are called one by one, in a set order, to participate with me in the stunt. A cat that happens to be hungry and craving a morsel of food from me will not wait until called to spring forward and try to win a goody. No, it will leave its perch the moment it de-cides it can wait no longer!

Thankfully, my cats are polite enough to sit patiently until it's time for their individual game with me, the conclusion of which earns them a tender caress and exclamation of, "Oh what a good kitty!" from their master.

With this new system in place, the little players in "Cat Skills" began showing off their talents consistently on stage—never mind the sea of people watching. The cats were fo-cused on showing their master just what they could do when he asked. And every time a cat's little game was completed, I immediately rewarded it with an appreciative pat and com-mending words. Perhaps the applause from the audience also registered in the cat's brain as a reward of sorts. That notion I can only guess at.

· · ·

SO YOU WANT TO begin training your own cat. Let me cover some essentials that will make this endeavor easier than trial-and-error.

I've found that teaching tricks is best with young cats up to three years old. Beyond that stage, their interest in playing games leading to their mastery of tricks begins to decline. There are exceptions, of course; I've trained cats as old as five years old. But if you're serious about mastering a trick with your pet cat, better to start with a willing kitten.

First, as mentioned before, carefully and patiently observe its habits. Does it constantly jump from one place to the next? Is it more of a frequent climber? Does it naturally bring objects to you and drop them at your feet? Does it prance and dart around your legs as you walk? This will clue you in to what kind of trick your cat can accomplish.

Second, keep in mind that a cat's attention span—at least as concerns playing a game with you—will last about five minutes. Therefore, that must be the length of your training session together. You'll discover this yourself. Teaching a cat to jump—it will follow your leads one, two, three, four times, maybe five times in a row. Then it will lose interest. But consistency is important, so plan on having two five-minute training sessions each day.

Third, try to do the training sessions at the same hour each day. You may discover that your cat will approach you to start the game. Make sure the cat is interested in playing, though. Need I remind you that you cannot force a cat to do anything it doesn't want to? All you can do is encourage it, and reward it when it does what you desire.

The game should begin very simply. If you want a cat to jump through a hoop, use a large hoop and don't hold it at a very great distance from the cat. Or if you want it to jump from chair to chair, position the chairs very close together at the start. And so on.

The visual cues should begin with a feather on a stick. Waving this will attract a cat's attention. It works as a good prompt to bring the cat into action. If you want a cat to jump from one chair to the next, you lead it with the feather (waving the feather in the spot you want your cat to jump) as you say, in an even tone, "C'mon, c'mon, c'mon . . ." At this point, the cat is thinking about jumping. Now you make sure to convince it to do so. You change your tone of voice into one that is firm and louder (though not so loud that it will startle or frighten the cat). "Jump!" you say. This final command is a prompt the cat will readily respond to, and remember for the next time.

Eventually, after this stunt is mastered with the feather, you can replace the feather with a wand. Later, you progress to scratching with a finger. Finally, all that's needed for a visual command is to point a finger until issuing the order, "Jump!" And the cat will follow.

Having finished its trick, reward the cat with, "Good, good kitty!" in your gracious, aggrandizing

Sebastian.

tone, coupled with a kind stroke on the head and back or maybe a tiny puckered kiss on its cheek.

Your tone returns to normal. "Now, sit down, sit down." And it returns to its perch, pleased with itself.

Use of a long feather as a physical cue works with other stunts. If you want a cat to move swiftly around your legs, making figure 8s between and around your feet as you walk, you begin by leading it with a feather, tapping each spot where you want it to go. Follow with the reward of praise. The feather is also used to set the cat into position for the fetching routine. Then you toss the object. Every time the cat returns the object to you, that's when you tell it how good a kitty it is.

As days and weeks go by, you gradually make the tricks more difficult, more complex—always respecting the cat's physical limitations. Never, ever, abandon your common sense by putting your pet at risk of injury, such as trying to train it to jump from a high shelf onto a bed.

Eventually you can perform the trick outside of the regular times of the training sessions. All that's required is the cat's responsiveness to your setting up the trick. If it joins you, you're ready to go!

AS MENTIONED MANY TIMES, every cat is a unique being, with its own personality, temperament, and peculiarities. So it stands to reason that your pet cat may be completely unwilling or unable to perform tricks.

In my act I use two cats whose great talent is doing absolutely nothing. I bring one of them on stage and set it on its own perch. I'll walk around, introducing the cats to the crowd. "This cat is talented at jumping," I'll say. "And this cat likes to climb. And *this* cat"—I'll point at the sedentary one—"is a special cat because, unlike all my other cats, she does nothing. And she does it very well!" This statement generates titters from the audience, among whom there always are plenty of cat owners who relate to the experience of living with a lazy cat whose chief activity is lounging for most of each day.

What if your cat proves to be very trainable, and you become a skilled duo performing tricks together, then one day it simply won't respond to your cues? You must accept that the trick is over before it's started. You'll have to try again another day. Even a cat that's always been eager to play along may, for whatever mysterious reason, not be in the right frame of mind one day and simply look away from you with complete lack of interest.

I have been regularly performing with cats on stage for more than a decade now, in front of thousands of people each week, with the best-trained domestic cats in the world. But these facts mean absolutely nothing to the 16 felines in the World Famous Popovich Comedy Pet Theater. That's why for every show I have two or even three cats I've prepared to perform a trick. This is my insurance against that uncomfortable moment when I approach a perched cat, gaze into its eyes, and instead of an animal alertly perking up, raising its ears and flicking its tail, communicating the message, "Take me, take me!", instantly ready for our game, I am met with a blasé or even vacant-headed cat staring back dully, silently bidding me to leave it be.

Fortunately, this lack of interest in one cat isn't contagious. It doesn't spread to the rest of the troupe. It's a numbers game for me. There always are enough happy cats that are wide awake, ready to go, eager to play with me and to garner their owner's grateful praise.

And so the show goes on.

. . .

SOMETIMES IF YOUR CAT begins losing interest in training for a trick, consider that maybe you need to up the reward. It's at least worth a try, instead of giving up. And since you may be the type of owner who constantly showers your cat with praise, you might find treats a stronger motivation, or perhaps scratching a particular favorite spot on its head or neck. Experiment with different rewards and see what your cat responds to best. I'm sure your pet won't mind being the subject of such attentions.

One of my female cats, Zita, had begun learning to leap through hoops. She was progressing beautifully . . . until one day in rehearsal she began playing around instead of jumping on cue. She walked around the chair, ignoring me. Then Zita finally decided to jump, and did so just fine. But from then on her cooperation was very unpredictable.

She would only jump when she wanted to, and it seemed nothing I did could encourage her to working with me as a team. Day after day, I didn't know what to expect from her. I was at wit's end, about ready to quit our training. I knelt over her, and distractedly scratched a spot on the back of her neck. All of a sudden Zita jumped through the hoop!

I realized in that instant that all she needed was a little bit more of an incentive to perform.

I built on this quirk, and soon we had a consistent routine mastered. In fact, I adapted it into her act on stage. I would place Zita on a chair and exhort her to jump through the hoop and land on the adjacent chair. The audience would laugh as she just sat still, ignoring me. So I'd lift her up and put her through the hoop and set her on the chair. This would bring more roars of laughter. Then I'd scratch the special spot on her back and—lo and behold—Zita would leap through the hoop back to the original chair, to giddy applause.

The popularity of this stunt proves a truth about the charm cats hold on us humans. We appreciate the fickleness, the headstrongness, the amusing unpredictability of cats as they continually demonstrate to their owners that a cat will do what it wants to do when it wants to do it, and there never really is a compromise.

Cats may be relatively small, and we may pretend that they are tame, but in their hearts they truly are still wild creatures. Wild and free. This is one of the main reasons why we humans so deeply admire cats and desire them as pets. We are attracted by their independence. They allow us to feed and house them. We marvel at our ability to get them to cooperate, to a degree, with the rules of our homes. And frankly, we are delighted when they bother granting us some affection in return.

When I first arrived in America as a veteran of the Great Moscow Circus, my mind-set was that of a juggler and acrobat who would wow the masses with feats of strength and speed, daring and dexterity. I was a young man who had captured trophies in international competitions. For me, the more fearless and gravity-defying I could make my act, the greater the applause and my fame would be. I was committed to amazing the American audiences. In my two-year tenure with the Ringling Bros. and Barnum & Bailey Circus, I focused on demonstrating my physical prowess. One highlight was balancing on a freestanding ladder while juggling nine rings. This feat earned me a world record.

A few years later, in the period when I was performing my combination juggler/clown act on the Midway at Circus Circus in Las Vegas, I hit on the idea of working cats into my act as a novelty that would set my performance apart from anything else. But I still had it in my mind that the more physically daunting the stunts were, the greater the applause would be, and the brighter the show-biz future for myself and my furry accomplices. I could train a cat to jump from a perch ten feet down onto my shoulder. And then 15 feet. And maybe even higher, if it were willing and I were able to catch it safely! And so on. It would take a tremendous amount of time and effort, but I'd build an act of astounding animal daredevils.

But this tack, I came to learn, was not what audiences wanted. I took my pet theater on the road, crisscrossing the country five times, hitting seemingly every city large and small along the way. And what drew the greatest applause were the humorous moments on stage when an animal made a delightful entrance or performed an adorable skit. I would work up a big sweat juggling an armful of rings, tossing them high, catching them in all kinds of crazy postures, and concluding with a backward somersault in the air. Night after night, this drew a reaction far less impressive than that given the dog, dressed as a master of ceremonies, walking up to a microphone to start off the show, and standing there as a deep voice we could imagine coming from the pooch (though really from a taped announcement) welcomed the audience to the show. And a cat on its hind legs pushing a dog in a baby buggy was pure gold, because it is not something you'd ever imagine seeing. And so, despite my ambitions to impress my audiences with my astounding physical feats, I was humbled by my furry costars, and the astounding love they drew from their audiences.

IN A MOMENT, I'll provide instructions for tricks you can teach your cat. When it comes to teaching your cat tricks, never ever overdo it. Never scold your pet over losing interest in the trick or not mastering it quickly enough. Never turn what should be a fun game into some sport to bolster your own ego. Never push the limits of safety. The animal's comfort level should be paramount in your interests.

The late French author Antoine de St. Exupéry, in his classic book *The Little Prince,* included this exchange between a fox and the title character:

"Men have forgotten this truth," said the fox. "But you must not forget it. You become responsible, forever, for what you have tamed."

SIX TRICKS YOU CAN TEACH YOUR CAT AT HOME

Here are six tricks for you to teach your cat at home. But before beginning, let me emphasize a few points mentioned in this chapter:

1) Observe your cat's physical habits and play off them.
2) Be patient. Tricks can take months to master. Just practice every day, and ideally at the same hour each day.
3) Never try forcing your cat to play when it doesn't want to, or make it play longer than it cares to. A reasonable length: five minutes at a time, and no more than two sessions a day. Longer than that, and the cat will lose attention, and the game will no longer be fun for it.
4) Never punish your cat for not performing a trick. If you ever yell at it, swat it or otherwise physically abuse it, this could mean the end of learning the trick forever. A cat will remember the negative experience and likely will refuse to play the game with you from then on.

5) Never put your cat at risk by leading it into a trick that strains or exceeds its physical abilities. That is a severe violation of the pact between owner and pet. Remember: You are responsible for this animal's welfare and wellbeing.

TRICK NUMBER ONE: JUMPING FROM CHAIR TO CHAIR

- Place two chairs facing each other, perhaps only a yard apart. Take a pet toy feather (a big bright feather on a long wand). Place the cat on one chair. Wave the feather around it to get its attention and start it playing with the feather.
- Now step to the other chair and wag the feather just above the seat to grab its attention. Encourage it to jump, calling its name. "Here, Bella." It will jump for the feather. Immediately after it lands, reward it with kind words—"good girl!" or the like—and hug, pat, or kiss it lovingly.
- Repeat the trick on the opposite chair and continue several more times. Every time it performs the trick, reward it.
- Each step of this trick can be repeated two days in a row before continuing on to the subsequent step.
- The next step in mastering this trick is moving the chairs slightly farther apart every two days until you finally have achieved an impressive, though safe, distance for the cat.
- At this point, turn the feather around and lead it into the trick each time with the handle point instead of the feather. It'll learn to follow the motion of your pointing, instead of the feather.
- Once this becomes automatic for it, get rid of the feather

toy entirely and instead use a finger. You can augment this prompt by scratching on the chair. You may have to reposition the cat if it lies down or turns away.

- When it masters this step, you have a cat that nimbly jumps from one chair to the next just with a finger point or feint of your hand.

TRICK NUMBER TWO: JUMPING THROUGH A HOOP

- Now that your cat has mastered jumping from one chair to the next, add a plastic hoop. Choose a relatively large hoop—one nearly the size of a hula hoop—so that the cat isn't intimidated. Hoops can be found at toy stores. Cut a hoop smaller and reattach ends as needed.
- Hold the hoop centered between the chairs, and at a height that doesn't cause the cat to leap any higher than when jumping from chair to chair. Give the cat a prompt, and it will jump through the hoop and land on the opposite chair. As always—reward it with happy praise and a hug, pat or satisfying scratch.
- The next step is using a smaller hoop, and raising it a tad higher.

TRICK NUMBER THREE: JUMPING THROUGH A HOOP WITH A PAPER CENTER

- Eventually you can have the cat jumping through a hoop with a paper center, so that she bursts through the paper. Very impressive! Most cats that perform trick number

Zita.

two can perform trick number three. All it takes is a little extra practice. As always, patience is key. Do not push your cat. Expect the trick to be mastered in one to two months.

- To train a cat to perform this trick, I cut a hoop to 17 to 19 inches in diameter. I then cut two 1-inch-wide strips of a soft paper towel (which is easily breakable) and stretch them across the hoop, one near the top and one near the bottom of the hoop, taping them with clear tape to the edges. The middle area, in other words, is spacious. The cat will usually jump through the hoop undeterred by the paper strips. To make the trick easier for the cat, move the landing chair slightly inward to minimize the gap between the chairs and make the jump easier.

- The cat will learn that the paper won't hurt it. After a few days of practice, I'll add two more strips, decreasing the opening by another inch at the top and the bottom.

- Continue adding strips every few days, until after several weeks, only half an inch remains in the center. It is important to leave this opening so that the cat can see where she's jumping. Finally, I reduce the opening to 1/4 inch. Once the trick is mastered, it will look very good to an audience — showing how brave your cat is.

TRICK NUMBER FOUR: JUMPING FROM CHAIR ONTO YOUR SHOULDER

- Wear an old jacket, sweater, or sweatshirt for this trick, since your clothes can get frayed. Make sure the clothing is thick enough to keep you from getting scratched. Do not cut your cat's claws, since it will need them for gripping.

- Place your cat on a chair and kneel or crouch close to it, facing it a couple feet away. Pick up the toy feather. Simply wave and tap the feather on your shoulder, get your cat's attention, and instead of it jumping to the other chair as before, it will jump onto your shoulder.
- Reward it as always with words and caresses. Replace it on the chair and repeat a few times.
- The next step is crouching a little taller, and then taller still, until you're standing up straight.
- The next step: Turn the feather around and point only with the wand. The following step: Use only your finger pointing. Eventually, just pointing your shoulder at your cat can prompt it to leap onto your shoulder.

TRICK NUMBER FIVE: JUMPING OVER BARRIERS

- Find out your cat's favorite place. Maybe it's an easy chair.
- When it's sitting there, gently take it off and place it on the floor. Then with the feather toy, tap the chair, and it'll jump back up on it. Reward it.
- Next, place a low barrier in front of the chair. The barrier can be a book (or two) opened up and standing upright, spine toward the ceiling. Or you can use a little board or a shoebox, or the like. Position the barrier about a yard from the chair.
- Lift your cat off its favorite chair, place it behind the barrier, and with the feather tapping in front of it direct it to return to its chair. It will jump over the barrier by

following the feather—and without even thinking about the barrier—so it can get to her chair. Reward it.

- Your next steps will be using the wand end of the feather, then your finger, and then using a higher barrier, and then adding a second barrier, and more as desired.

- Eventually your cat will be hurdling over barriers and leaping up to the designated chair, *any* chair, following your pointed finger.

TRICK NUMBER SIX: WALKING AROUND YOUR LEGS

- Crouch by your cat and wave the feather around, gaining the cat's attention so it follows the feather. Then stand up, hunched over, with your legs parted. With the feather, lead the cat between your legs once. Reward it.

- Next goal: Take one step forward and lead the cat again through your legs, from the other side.

- Soon it will be following you for four or five steps.

- Next: Turn the feather backward and lead it with the wand end. Next: With your finger.

- Eventually, it won't need any prompt. Just your walking.

- As always: Reward your cat at the end of the trick.

🐾 PAW PRINTS 🐾

- You can only train a cat to do a trick if it is naturally inclined to the physical act in question. A training game must be based around its habit of climbing, fetching, jumping, or walking around legs.

- A cat performs only if it wants to, not just because you want it to. Punishment for not accomplishing a trick is wrong, and entirely ineffective.

- Unlike dogs, most cats respond better to rewards of pats and praise rather than receiving edible treats. A key to training a cat to do tricks is to reserve your most effusive praise and loving strokes as prizes for performing a trick, instead of for ordinary acts during the day.

- Cats that have a close connection with their owners yearn to please their owners, yet don't know how. Performing tricks that make their masters happy give cats an avenue for doing something nice for their human providers.

- The human voice can have a hypnotic effect on cats. The kind, soft, nearly singing, "What a good kitty!" can lull a cat into contentment. This phrase of praise is a heady reward for it, indeed.

- A training session should be no longer than five minutes at a time. Try to train twice a day.

- A feather is an ideal physical cue with which to begin training a cat to follow your directions. Eventually you can substitute a wand, then your finger, and, finally, just a finger point.

- If your cat begins losing interest in performing a trick that it previously did with no problem, and you don't want to give up, one possibility is rewarding it even more with your strokes and praise, and maybe a loving scratch in a spot it likes, and seeing if it will respond.

18

Growing Older with Your Cat

"There are two means of refuge from the misery of life—
music and cats."
—ALBERT SCHWEITZER

In the troupe of furry performers of the World Famous Popovich Comedy Pet Theater are three veteran cats that have put in a dozen years of service on stage. As they reached their advanced ages, I noticed they began more frequently to decline to perform tricks on cue; therefore, I increasingly gave them passes to stay put on their perches while I engaged younger alternates in the various routines.

Finally, I decided to leave this mature trio behind in their home cages when I loaded up the team of performers for transport to the theater and the late-afternoon show. I didn't anticipate the reaction of these veterans. At the sight of their comrades being carried off to the truck without them, they began pacing wildly, pawing at their cage walls, yowling, very upset.

This tore at my heart! I decided on a compromise: I loaded them up with the others, but instead of bringing them on stage to their accustomed posts, I left them in the dressing room. Even this wasn't enough to please the cats entirely. Sometimes, as I get into my costume before a performance, one of these cats will walk up to me on the table and rub against me, as if saying, "I want to get out there, just like old times, and jump through the ring." And guess what? I'll let it take its turn in its old role yet again.

The cat invariably will carry off the stunt just like when it was younger. It proves "there's still some gunpowder in the old barrel yet," as a Russian proverb goes.

It makes me proud that even my oldest cat performers aren't content to simply lounge on sofas and enjoy a lazy retirement. Perhaps the force of longstanding habit, of drives to the theater year after year, is too deeply ingrained in their beings. Or maybe—since my performers were rescued from animal shelters in kittenhood—that early fear of being abandoned, left behind in sudden solitude while their mates go to the show, impels them to protest being left behind.

Sebastian and Masha.

And so I bring them along to the theater, knowing full well they'll probably just stay put in the dressing room while the show goes on.

Perhaps in years ahead, as these old pros grow more advanced in their years, they may decide to stay behind at home. As their loving and faithful master, I intend to heed whatever requests they make in this regard.

A CAT WITH WHICH you've developed a very close connection can sense your mood and know when to approach you or avoid you. If it decides you'd enjoy it hanging out with you—say, if you're feeling a little blue, or tired—the animal won't come up to you right away. It will need time to scan you and determine your state of mind. But then it will approach.

Two of my older cats, in particular, will come over to me when I'm sitting at the computer or reading. They see me, perhaps, as being a bit too absorbed in my solitude. They'll come behind my chair and sit there, just to keep me company. This I appreciate!

Many cat owners have experienced instances when they've been feeling sad or depressed, and lo and behold, the pet cat, with a concerned expression, will come up and nuzzle against them. It perceives its duty as comforting you when you especially need some tender loving care.

In the World Famous Popovich Comedy Pet Theater I perform rigorous juggling stunts, and end one routine with a backward somersault in the air. Sometimes I experience back pain, especially if the floor of the theater where I'm performing is particularly hard.

At home, I'll call Gypsy, one of my older cats. I'll be sitting at my chair, working on a computer. She'll come into the room, jump up on the chair where I point, and nestle in behind me, a warm cushion for my back. She's like a longhaired, black-and-white, living heating pad. She is fine with helping me this way.

My mother, Tamara, suffered a stroke. She told me that when she felt high blood pressure, she'd call her cat, and it would come and lie behind her head where it rested on a pillow. This lowered my mother's stress, stabilizing her blood pressure.

Such are the therapeutic powers of a pet cat. It's not just a one-way street, the owner providing for the animal's welfare. The animal can keep the owner healthy, too. You can ease the aging process together.

WHILE WE CHERISH OUR PETS, the sad fact is that nothing lasts forever, and we are prone to outlive our cats. A well-provided-for cat that has received proper diet and health care will live on the average of 14 years. Some don't live that long; others live much longer.

In general, a cat starts showing signs of old age at eight to nine years. Unlike with people, you won't notice graying or whitening hair or the appearance of wrinkles. Rather, you'll notice teeth yellowing (although this can occur at a young age). Sometimes an older cat's teeth fall out. When a cat has reached a very advanced age, its fatty layers will disappear from its spine and around its eyes. The cat will take on a leaner appearance.

Elderly cats require special care. Their sense of smell declines, and they are prone to eat less, unable to sniff the food as before, which affects their appetite. (One solution to getting your cat to eat more is putting pungent food such as fish or cheese in its bowl. While fish isn't recommended for younger cats, it may help keep an elderly cat up to a healthy weight.) Aged cats must be fed more than twice a day, although the overall daily portions don't change. Three or four meals that would have equaled the intake of two meals before are the norm. If the cat normally ate its largest meal in the evening, continue that routine. Cats are great creatures of habit.

You should limit the aged cat's consumption of red meat, replacing it with white meat such as poultry and fish. Vitamin supplements are recommended. For very old cats, food should be ground into pulp.

Elderly cats greatly dislike changes in their living situations. They don't respond well to strangers, or in alterations of the home, such as furniture moved around. An addition of a new pet at this stage is not advised.

Aged cats need daily combing of their fur—an aid to the cat's decrease in washing itself, given its declining energy. Cats crave cleanliness, so this daily grooming will prove therapeutic to your pet. Along with combing the fur, wipe the cat's muzzle and eyes with a moist sponge.

Older cats lose their spryness, and frequently suffer from arthritis, poor blood circulation, urinary problems, and kidney disease, just like older humans. Their body temperature lowers, and they seek out warm places. They sleep more. Their fur loses its thickness and luster. They become more susceptible to diseases such as diabetes.

Many illnesses associated with advanced age develop gradually and, at first, are imperceptible to the owner. Cats, as said before in this book, are stoic by nature, concealing their discomfort and pain.

An old cat requires special attention and care. As a cat owner, you have dutifully provided for your pet's quality of life and happiness, and it has returned it with its devotion and love. If now, in the twilight of its life, it contracts an illness and is suffering too much, the most humane option may be putting it to sleep.

PROPER CARE BY YOU, the owner, is a huge factor in guaranteeing the longevity of your cat. To be sure, other factors come into play: including the cat's genetics, and luck in not contracting a serious disease or being injured or killed in an accident. As previously mentioned, a neutered cat that has received good veterinary care can be expected to live for about 14 years. But a cat that has been well provided for, given an optimal diet, safe environment, and health care, may live into its late teens or early twenties.

There are different guides for comparing a cat's age to those of a human. One that makes sense to me is to consider that a 1-year-old cat is equivalent in age span to a 15-year-old human. Add another nine years for the second year: meaning that a 2-year-old cat is about 24 in human years. Then add four more human years for each subsequent cat year. Therefore, a 14-year-old cat is 72 in human years.

Outside of annual visits to the vet, you must be the one to monitor your cat's health. This responsibility will require closer examinations, as the animal ages, to check for signs of health woes.

Monthly bath times are conducive to running a quick health exam of your cat; but whenever you give your cat a look-over, make sure it's done on a regular basis.

Check the cat's weight
Feel its ribs. Clasp your palms over the cat's sides. You should be able to feel the edges poking under a thin layer of fat. Too much girth, or too little, are indications of an unhealthy cat. You should consult with a vet on changes in the cat's diet, and (if it is too thin) presence of ailments.

Check the fur and skin
The fur must appear shiny and feel smooth to the touch as you run your hand from head to tail. Dull-looking or jumbled fur indicates a poor diet or an illness. Separate the fur on the head and along the spine, looking for signs of insect bites, peelings or wounds. Look along the base of the tail and the stomach for the dark clusters that show the presence of fleas.

Check the eyes
Verify that the lower lid of each eye is pink. The whites of the eyes must not show reddening. The pupils should shrink in size when exposed to a light source. Check the eyes for dark spots, which can be a sign of infection.

Check the ears
The insides must be clean and light pink, free of a bad odor and of the dark, coffee ground–like substances that indicate mites.

Check the teeth
Check for inflamed gums and cracked or missing teeth. Older cats often loose teeth. This can make chewing more difficult and also cause serious health problems if bacteria from oral infections spread to the bloodstream.

☸ PAW PRINTS ☸

- A well-tended cat lives on average 14 years.
- In general, a cat shows signs of old age at 8 to 9 years.
- Signs of advanced age include teeth yellowing or falling out, and fatty layers disappearing from the spine and around the eyes.
- Special care for elderly cats includes feeding it more often, reducing red meat, adding vitamin supplements, combing its fur and wiping its face daily.

Conclusion

An Afternoon of Comedy Pet Theater

"He who dislikes the cat was in his former life a rat."
—Chinese proverb

It is a weekday afternoon on the Las Vegas Strip, the entertainment epicenter of the world. The brightest stars in show business have their names emblazoned on the towering marquees fronting the most famous mega-casinos on Earth. Forty million visitors a year, from six of the seven continents, come to Vegas to soak up the 24-hour excitement. Among the hordes of fun-seekers are not only those bent on gambling, nurturing the age-old fantasy of a jackpot courtesy of Lady Luck's caprice, but families with wide-eyed children marveling at the themed resorts, state-of-the-art amusement parks, Oz-like atmosphere and unforgettable stage shows.

From the wealthiest of the "whales"—the highest of the

high rollers treated as royalty, their penthouse suites and gourmet feasts "comped" by their casino hosts—to the humblest of working folk taking advantage of bargain room rates and budget-friendly buffets, they're all seeking sensational thrills and lasting memories in this immense playground of casino castles, whose nighttime neon dazzles in a rainbow spectrum of rich hues.

Las Vegas. The name itself casts a magical spell on tourists. And on entertainers, too. As a stage performer, whether you headline in the grandest showroom or ply your profession in a little lounge, if you're playing Vegas, baby, it means you have attained a high level of proficiency, and you maintain a consistent standard of excellence. It means you have arrived. You know a good-size audience will be at your show. You know the attendees will be expecting not only to be entertained, but delighted and surprised. They have entered an enchanted amusement zone, here on the Strip. They are riding a wave of excitement that lifted them up the moment they landed at McCarran International Airport or motored out of the stark desert into the grid of the great metropolis sprawling in the Las Vegas Valley. Your job is to keep them surfing along, to give them something special to applaud—and then to laugh at, or gasp at, and applaud even harder.

It's just a few minutes before four o'clock at the V Theater, an ornate 400-seat showroom with pillared arches, tucked into a corner of the enormous Miracle Mile Shops, which is connected to the Planet Hollywood Resort & Casino. The retail promenade has 170 stores and kiosks and 15 restaurants, all under a towering ceiling painted with white clouds and blue sky that gives the impression of being outdoors. Outside the theater, a line of eager show-goers of all ages snakes from the ticket counter and out into the mall's corridor, opposite an Italian restaurant. Inside the theater, backstage, I'm dressed in my clown's outfit of baggy brown trousers, over-sized black boots, a tattered black tunic, checkered vest, red bowtie and wide-brimmed red hat. My pancake makeup is brushed on, cheeks and chin dotted with blush, lips red-dened, eyelids blued, eye rims and eyelashes blackened, the tip of my nose beaming a bright crimson.

Right on cue, adrenaline surges through my body. This feeling of nervousness mingled with glee never goes away. It is part of a performer's addiction to the stage. I have spent my entire life in show business. I grew up in a circus family. My great-grandparents, grandparents and parents all made their living under the big top. Today I am founder and pro-ducer of the World Famous Popovich Comedy Pet Theater. My act is regularly engaged five afternoons a week at the V Theater, except when touring. If you include all the dates that the Comedy Pet Theater has played around the nation and in 25 countries, the number of people who've seen my show in person exceeds 1 million. Millions more have watched my cats perform their tricks on television on *The To-night Show*, *Late Night with David Letterman*, *America's Got Talent*, and other programs in the United States, Europe, and Japan. I've also produced a series of three DVDs featuring the various animal segments of Comedy Pet Theater.

But there is nothing better than performing in front of a live audience, just as there is no complete substitute for see-ing a show live, rather than on a screen. As my cohorts and I make our final preparations backstage, the bustle and buzz of the attendees as they take their seats in the darkened theater is electric. All the cast members of Comedy Pet Theater feel this vibrant energy. Including the animals.

I make my final rounds of the dressing rooms, looking in,

asking if everyone's ready, informing them the show will start in two minutes. "We have a good crowd!" I say. I squeeze my fists and give a "let's go!" pump of confidence—playing the part of the combination producer/stage director. Among the dressing rooms is one reserved just for the dogs, and another for the cats. As usual right before a show, the animals are perched on chairs or tables, alert and obedient, feeling at ease in the company of their longtime comrades. The separation of species is only temporary. Soon, dogs and cats will be mingling on stage—along with rats, doves, and ferrets, human acrobats and clowns. My wife, Izolda, will perform her quick-change costume routine. Our daughter, Anastasia, will wow the crowd by juggling balls and limberly spinning 30 hula hoops. I will clamber up a freestanding ladder, juggle pins, catch and stack tossed pans and blocks, and perform Chaplinesque sketches with my trained animals, delivering my very best clown personas.

But I know that, as always—and as it should be—the greatest cheers will come for the dogs and cats, dressed in colorful bibs or collars, earnestly carrying out their roles in the humorous skits and unexpected stunts.

This is, after all, "Comedy Pet Theater."

IT'S SHOWTIME! On tall screens set up on opposite sides of the stage, a slideshow of still photos, "Gregory's Home Movies," gives a quick history of the show, with the narration explaining that each trained cat and dog was rescued from an animal shelter. The audio includes my pitch encouraging people who are seeking a pet to visit an animal shelter, and to have their adoptees spayed or neutered, to prevent needless litters that fill shelters with pets that never are claimed.

The slideshow ends and the stage production lights come up, shining a bluish-purple sheen. Sequins glitter against a black backdrop. Calliope music booms on the sound system. Cats begin walking quickly in each direction across four tightropes crisscrossing the stage. An announcer's recorded voice, like Sylvester the Cat's, says, "Suffering succotash. C'mon, hurry up and move! Let's go, let's go, we're going to be late for the show! Gregory's already called for us! C'mon, let's go! Move on slowpoke, move on!"

As the last cat disappears off stage, a spotlight shines on stage left, where a golden retriever, who happens to be seven-year-old Jerry, appears behind a podium. He is wearing a gray suit coat and big red bowtie. He moves his dog's muzzle up to an old-style microphone. A deep voice that sounds like it would belong to him pipes over the public-address system: "Ladies and gentlemen, please welcome the Comedy Pet Theater, by Gregory Popovich!"

The crowd erupts in applause. The mood is set.

And for the next hour, circus skills and slapstick gags take turns on stage—alternately making attendees giggle, bust up, or cheer in appreciation or sheer amazement.

I make my entrance in my clown outfit, wearing my red hat. I juggle sticks. A dog carries a basket full of balls to me. I balance the basket and the dog on a pole, the dog dropping balls and I shooting them back up to the basket.

I juggle five pins while balanced on a freestanding ladder. I toss rings overhead, catching them in my hands or around my neck. I nab pans as they are tossed at me. I sandwich blocks flung at me. But enough of me. It's the animals the audience wants to see.

In my ringmaster getup with red-and-black brocaded suit coat, black satin pants, high leather boots, and top hat, I face my dozen-plus feline performers, each standing or crouching on a stool topped with red fringed red cloth. I invite one cat at a time to perform. It bounds off its perch.

Misha, a nine-year-old cat with orange head, back and tail and white body, faces the hoop I hold up. It is covered with paper. He leaps through, bursting the paper. But he isn't finished. Two parallel poles are balanced between two tall barstools. A disco ball is balanced between the poles. Misha climbs on the ball and with little kicks propels the ball along the poles, never falling off. Then, by himself, the game cat hangs by his forepaws on the poles, and shimmies along to the end, then slides down the stand.

Sugar, a five-year-old all-white beauty, cinches up a ten-foot-high pool to a little platform, and on my command leaps all the way down, alighting cleanly and safely on my shoulder.

The audience has never seen anything like that!

The dogs get their moments, too. In a classroom setting, a dozen pooches sit at desks aligned in three rows. I stand before them in a professorial cap and gown.

"I would like to ask a math question," I say. "Wait a second, the board is dirty. I need someone to clean the board."

A white poodle mix in red shorts and red gloves walks up and paws the board clean.

As soon as my back is turned, a little brown-and-white shaggy mutt comes up and tugs my chair away. As I squat to sit, I hit the floor. I pick up the chair, and a white heeler with black face and a white stripe down his front comes up and gives me a shove from behind, toppling me again.

I call on Jerry, the golden retriever who was the emcee at the beginning of the show. He steps out of his seat on his hind legs. I ask him, "How much is 3 plus 2?"

He barks thrice, then twice.

"Very good, go back to your seat."

I spin a big blue globe. "Now a geography question. Who would like to show me where is the Pacific Ocean?"

I call Rudy the boxer. He leaves his desk and on his back legs walks up to the front and places a paw on the expanse of blue, representing the Pacific, on the globe.

"Very good," I say. I shake his paw.

THERE IS A LITTLE subplot in the show, and it serves to bring in Comedy Pet Theaters' two most popular stars.

In the role of a hapless clown, I am trying to join a circus, but I mess up too often and am booted from the show by the other clowns. I become a traveling vagabond.

The stage setting is a dark winter night in an empty park. Next to a bench stands an old-fashioned light pole. A cat appears, and shimmies up the pole to a platform between three gas lanterns. This is five-year-old Sebastian, a beautiful, lean, shorthaired creature with a striped, cream-colored body patched with white on his breast, feet, and tail tip. His opal eyes peer keenly down as I appear, lumbering along, a forlorn character in an overcoat, carrying a tattered umbrella. I take a seat on the bench as mournful accordion and flute music plays in the background.

From my coat I bring out a sausage link and set it on a plate. Unbeknownst to me, a dog pops out of a wastebasket behind me to my left. This is Rex, a three-year-old schnauzer with white body, charcoal-colored back and rear, and whiskey head and ears. Rex snatches the sausage, then bounds back into the basket. When I see the plate is empty, I am shocked. I produce another sausage . . . and catch Rex in the act of trying to pilfer it, too.

Elated for any company in my wretched existence, I set out a dish for him. He comes and eats from it. We make friends as I hug him. But a policeman, in tall hat and long overcoat, comes and rousts me away. The cat meows, and I beckon him to join us. Down he comes from the lamppost. The three of us leave together.

The spectators soon find out that Rex and Sebastian are great friends. The duo account for the two biggest highlights of the show. Rex is sitting in a baby buggy and Sebastian comes up behind it, rises onto his rear legs, and with forelegs draped over the handle, walks forward, pushing the buggy across the stage, to oohs and ahs from the audience.

Later, Sebastian crouches behind Rex then leaps onto the pooch's back. Rex lifts up onto his hind legs and gives his feline pal a piggyback ride across the stage, finally lowering himself as I scoop him up. Sebastian leaps onto my shoulder.

Another exciting climax to a surprising animal feat. Another lesson, too, about the hidden talents of pets.

Rex and Sebastian get their rewards in the form of the audience's applause—and in their owner's exclamations of pride and pleasure in them, accompanied by his loving strokes.

AFTER THE SHOW, the audience files out, hundreds of happy faces. As they gather in lines to the exit, the Comedy Pet Theater's human players stand to a side, waving good-bye. Many patrons pause long enough to purchase a show DVD. The most eager fans, though, line up for a great treat: a photograph with one of the stars.

Not with me, Gregory Popovich. Nor with any of my other talented human troupe members.

But with one of our cats.

As I mentioned in Chapter Six, the job of photo-op model belongs to Zuzu. Stout like a puffball, she is friendly and mellow, never minding the stream of children and adults who parade one by one up to her to pet her downy white fur mottled with caramel patches on head and back. My daughter will hold Zuzu next to the patron as the dignified cat calmly and patiently looks at the camera lens pointed by Max, one of my assistants.

"One . . . two . . . *three!*" then flash.

And a memorable Las Vegas moment is captured forever.

About the Author

Gregory Popovich, a native of Kiev, Ukraine, is an alumnus of the Great Moscow Circus and the Ringling Bros. and Barnum & Bailey Circus; a trained clown and a world record–holding juggler; and founder of the World Famous Popovich Comedy Pet Theater. The show's cast includes 20 domestic cats and 16 dogs—each of which once was a stray rescued from an animal shelter. Popovich himself trains these animals to jump rope and leap through hoops, balance on hind legs, and perform in humorous sketches. His award-winning, family-oriented act also includes his unique comedy and juggling, and performances by European-style clowns and balancing acts.

Popovich's Comedy Pet Theater has performed in 25 countries and been featured on television's *The Tonight Show*, *Late Night with David Letterman*, *The Late Late Show with Craig Ferguson*, Animal Planet, and *America's Got Talent* (on which Popovich was a finalist in 2007). Comedy Pet Theater also has been written about in *People* magazine, *The New York Times Sunday Magazine*, the *Los Angeles Times*, and the *New*

Yorker. While periodically touring, the Comedy Pet Theater is based at the V Theater inside the Miracle Mile Shops, at Planet Hollywood Resort & Casino, in Las Vegas. (For information on tour dates, tickets and DVDs, plus videos and pictures of the show, go to www.comedypet.com.)

Popovich resides in Las Vegas with his wife, Izolda, and their daughter, Anastasia, who also perform in the act. The Popoviches' extended family in Las Vegas numbers more than 50 furry or feathered members, which not only include cats and dogs but also ferrets and white mice, geese and doves.

You CAN Train Your Cat is Popovich's first book.